the outskirts of hope

A MEMOIR OF THE 1960s DEEP SOUTH

Jo Ivester

SOUTHLAND

"In the sixties, a lot of people talked the talk about civil rights. The Kruger family lived the life. This sensitive but no-holds-barred account of their life in Mound Bayou, Mississippi is one of the most gripping real-life stories of confronting and dealing with racism ever written. Warning: Once you start reading *The Outskirts of Hope*, you won't be able to stop."

—Forrest Preece, columnist, *West Austin News*

"This is a fascinating tale of a family who took their three youngest children to an essentially all-black community in the Mississippi Delta, where the father opened a medical clinic and the mother taught in an all-black school. The kids survived, albeit not without drama."

—Dave Richards, lawyer,
US Civil Rights Commissioner in the 1960s

"An unflinching memoir of the hopes, triumphs, and disappointments of a white family that moves to a black community in one of the most segregated areas of the American South in the late 1960s. This engaging book offers a rare and moving narrative of the power of seemingly modest personal activities in delivering the durable social changes promised by laws and policy."

—Bob Flanagan, Professor Emeritus, Stanford University

"Ivester's Jewish-Bostonian family took a chance on the importance of being human at a time when life was minimized based on the color of a person's skin. Ivester captures the essence of the resulting journey through the dual eyes of a child and her mother as they learn the impact of just saying yes."

—Gigi Edwards Bryant,
Trustee, Austin Community College District

THE

OUTSKIRTS

of

HOPE

To Valerie – Thanks for getting it.

Best Always,

[signature]

Published 2015
Printed in the United States of America
ISBN: 978-1-63152-964-1
Library of Congress Control Number: 2014953583

Book design by Stacey Aaronson

For information, address:
She Writes Press
1563 Solano Ave #546
Berkeley, CA 94707

She Writes Press is a division of SparkPoint Studio, LLC.

THE

OUTSKIRTS

of

HOPE

BY

JO IVESTER

Based on the journals of her mother,
Aura Kern Kruger

For teachers everywhere

Many Americans live on the outskirts of hope, some because of their poverty and some because of their color, and all too many because of both. Our task is to help replace their despair with opportunity.

—LYNDON B. JOHNSON,
ANNOUNCING THE WAR ON POVERTY, JANUARY 8, 1964

CONTENTS

PHOTOGRAPHS

CHAPTER ONE

Map of Mound Bayou, drawn by Mike Morgenfeld

Photo: Roadside shacks typical of Mississippi in the 1960s.

CHAPTER TWO

Photo: A shack in Mound Bayou.

CHAPTER THREE

Photo: The home the Krugers left when they moved to Mississippi.

CHAPTER FOUR

Photo: The trailers where the Krugers lived in Mound Bayou.

CHAPTER FIVE

Photo: From the 1967–68 John F. Kennedy High School year-book showing Aura teaching her English class (lower picture).

CHAPTER SIX

Photo: Jo (11) with her brothers, Charles (12) and Philip (14)

CHAPTER SEVEN

Photo: The unheated shacks were miserable when snow arrived.

CHAPTER EIGHT

Photo: Shacks lining the road.

CHAPTER NINE

Photo: Faculty picture of Aura from the 1967–68 JFK High yearbook.

CHAPTER TEN

Photo: Another example of Mississippi poverty.

CHAPTER ELEVEN

Opening Photo: Jo (11) with her parents, Aura and Leon Kruger.

Closing Photo: The road leading away from Mound Bayou.

CHAPTER TWELVE

Photo: Highway sign crossing from Tennessee to Mississippi. Taken by Elizabeth Norman.

PROLOGUE

My parents were foot soldiers in President Johnson's War on Poverty. One of the president's first actions after announcing his new program in 1964 was to send his lieutenants in search of the poorest spot in the country. Expecting to find it in Appalachia, they were surprised to discover it instead in the cotton fields of Mississippi.

By 1967, with a fresh new degree in public health, my pediatrician father decided to enlist. During the height of the civil rights movement, my family moved to a small, all-black town in the heart of the Mississippi Delta, where my father opened a clinic and my mother Aura Kruger, taught English at the local high school. I was the only white student at my junior high.

Both my mother and I kept journals of our time in Mound Bayou. Hers is the basis of the true story you are about to read. I burned mine decades ago because I was embarrassed by all that happened and couldn't imagine ever wanting to share my story. Reading my mother's journals, I was surprised how vividly and completely those memories came back. More than that, I was pleased to discover that I could almost reconstruct what I'd written as a child. Some of these re-creations are included here.

In a few cases, I have changed the names of individuals involved to respect and protect their privacy.

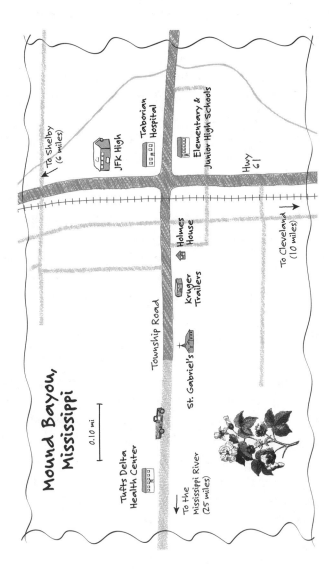

Mound Bayou, Mississippi

0.10 mi

Tufts Delta
Health Center

To the
Mississippi River
(25 miles)

St. Gabriel's

Township Road

Kruger
Trailers

Holmes
House

To Cleveland
(10 miles)

To Shelby
(6 miles)

JFK High

Taborian
Hospital

Elementary &
Junior High Schools

Hwy
61

ONE

❧

THE OUTSKIRTS *of* HOPE

Any person who shall be guilty of
circulating written matter presenting
for public acceptance suggestions in
favor of social equality between whites
and negroes, shall be subject to a fine
not exceeding five hundred (500.00)
dollars or imprisonment not exceeding
six (6) months or both.

—EXCERPT FROM MISSISSIPPI'S JIM CROW LAWS

March 1967
Aura (44 years old)

"Y ou ride in front," said John as he held the car door open for me.

Thinking he was just being polite, I answered, "Don't be silly. My legs are so short that I won't notice the difference."

"This isn't a choice, Aura. It's dangerous if I sit with Leon."

"Dangerous?"

"The Jim Crow laws. If a white person is driving, blacks have to sit in back." John Hatch, a community organizer who was working with my husband, Leon, to open a medical clinic in the Mississippi Delta, said this as if it were the most obvious thing in the world.

Then John added, "We don't want the Klan to notice us."

My mouth grew dry and I shivered, even though it was a warm April day. Suddenly, everything I'd read about life in the Deep South became personal. We could be in danger.

Once we were on the road, everyone sat silently. I longed for Leon's usual playfulness—his silly made-up songs, his stories about the places we passed, his excitement over where we were going. Perhaps he was as disturbed by John's warnings as I had been and was feeling just as tense. I used to be able to guess exactly what was going through his head without his having to tell me. After twenty-five years of marriage, we often knew each other's thoughts better than we did our own. But in the four weeks since Leon had unilaterally decided to move to Mississippi, a wall had grown between us. I ached to tell him of my fears, but he didn't want to hear about them. So—like the good wife I always aspired to be —I kept quiet.

As we drove south on Highway 61 toward the Mississippi state line, the road curved through pine forests almost as lovely as those I'd grown up with in New England, and the gently rolling terrain reminded me of the hills outside Boston. *This won't be so bad*, I told myself as I looked out the car window at the lush landscape.

Mound Bayou, where we were heading, was the oldest all-black town in the country. It would be the site of Leon's new clinic, which would serve the black population of Bolivar County. My husband, with such a big responsibility and so willing to help others. While I loved that in him, his decision meant that after spending most of my forty-four years in the Boston area, I now had to say good-bye to the life I loved, its theater and dinner parties, summers at the beach, and outstanding schools for my three young children. We would be one of two white families among the 1,300 people of Mound Bayou, and our presence alone would throw us into the heart of the civil rights movement.

I sat up taller so I could see better out the window. At only four foot ten, I had to strain to peer over the dashboard. Glancing at Leon behind the wheel, I appreciated how he'd never seemed to mind my being so short. Even back in high school, he'd just said I was cute. I think he actually preferred it, because it made him feel bigger. We fit together perfectly, especially when we danced, which we did as often as we could. Others would clear the dance floor as he'd twirl me about in the most intricate of moves. I wondered if there would be anywhere to dance in Mound Bayou.

At the Mississippi border, a billboard greeted us with a picture of a breathtaking antebellum mansion surrounded by magnolia trees. It said WELCOME TO MISSISSIPPI, THE MAGNOLIA STATE. Moments later, the road transitioned from a well-maintained highway to a bumpy two-lane blacktop. Then we rounded a curve and the trees disappeared, the road straightened, and the hills vanished. As far as the eye could see, there was nothing but mud. John explained that cotton had already been planted and would soon break through the surface. But for now, the mud reached to the horizon. We had entered the true Mississippi. My heart felt heavy. Even the air felt heavy.

All that broke the monotony were a few deserted shacks—at least I *thought* they were deserted, until I saw smoke coming from a chimney; scrawny, half-naked children playing in a yard; and tattered sheets hanging from a clothesline. It was like the scenes of third-world countries in *National Geographic* pictures.

Leon, as if reading my mind, said, "This is why we're moving, Aura. Somebody has to help. If we don't, who will?" When I tried to respond, my throat was so tight that no words came out. I knew he was right, but why did it have to be now, when our children were so young? Why did it have to be us?

We drove for another twenty miles, and nothing changed. Then another twenty. I passed the time thinking about the children. Had Philip, my seventh grader, finished his homework, as he had promised he would, before going to the school dance? Jo and Charles had planned on walking to the science museum. I cringed at the thought of them finding their way around downtown alone; they were only nine and ten years old and had never gone by themselves before. I'd agreed only because I knew that soon they'd be leaving Boston far behind.

Saddened at the thought, I made myself think instead about what John had said over dinner last night. Although tall and heavyset, John spoke softly, his constant smile providing comfort as he described the early planning of the health center, going back to 1964. As a cornerstone to his War on Poverty, President Johnson had sent Senator Robert Kennedy and Harvard's Robert Coles in search of the worst poverty in the country, expecting them to find it in Appalachia. Everyone was surprised to discover that living conditions were even worse in the Mississippi Delta, where the average annual family income was under $100 and people were starving.

Not long after that, Jack Geiger, a Mississippi field coordinator for a group that recruited medical personnel to support the Freedom Riders as they traveled the South registering blacks to vote, sought federal money to evaluate the feasibility of creating a community health center in the Delta. When he approached the new federal Office of Economic Opportunity for funding, he was so persuasive that he obtained enough money not just for a study, but also for the clinic itself.

John Hatch convinced Jack that Mound Bayou would be the perfect location for the new clinic. One hundred miles south of Memphis, it was considered a safe haven, unique in that all the property within the town limits was owned by its black residents and had been since its inception in 1887.

Landownership was critical in the post–Civil War South, for without it, the best that an uneducated black person could hope for was to be a sharecropper, planting and picking cotton on someone else's land. Because the people of Mound Bayou were property owners, a middle class was able to emerge. It was small, and by most people's standards poor, but Mound Bayou was proud of its success. The town had its own mayor and post office and, most important, its own school system. Children received a better education as a result, and a higher percentage learned to read and finished high school. Several of the residents even earned college degrees, something rare in Mississippi in the mid-1960s.

The town also housed the Taborian Hospital, which served the black population for miles around. White physicians in the segregated hospitals in neighboring towns often refused to treat blacks, or at least made them wait outside until the end of the day. State code even mandated that hospitals have separate entrances for blacks. Many of the physicians who did treat black patients were so uncomfortable with it that all they would do was ask questions; they wouldn't conduct a physical exam. In Mound Bayou, that wasn't an issue.

Nor was the Ku Klux Klan as much of a concern there as it was elsewhere. Locating the clinic in an all-black town offered some protection against dangers such as arson attacks and bombings. But it would still be hazardous. John had talked about the Klan the night before, describing some of the dangers inherent in life in the Deep South, troubles that he had faced growing up black and that we would face as outsiders trying to help. It was actually against the law for us to do anything to promote racial equality; we could get six months in jail just for trying.

I hated that Leon was pulling our family into a place where I'd have to be concerned about our children's safety. But I worried that if I told him I didn't want to move, he'd go alone and leave us behind. Even in the early days of our marriage, I was afraid that one day he would desert me —I wasn't pretty or smart enough, and I was too shy.

The more I fretted about the situation, the more tense I became, and I realized that I'd never last the whole two hours to Mound Bayou without a restroom break. It wasn't long before I felt desperate, anxiously watching for a glimmer of a gas station or a restaurant. "There's not even a tree for me to hide behind," I joked, trying to ignore the increasingly unpleasant sensation in my bladder.

At one point, the sight of a town in the distance raised my hopes, but it turned out to be just a few shacks clustered together, with a pile of junked cars nearby. I had begun to think that squatting by the side of the road where everyone could see would be preferable to waiting any longer when we finally spotted what looked to be an abandoned gas station. It was completely deserted—no other cars, no staff. *Please, please let it be unlocked, and let there be a bathroom,* I said to myself. Moments later, I sighed with relief as Leon stopped in front of the dilapidated building and I saw a sign that read WOMEN. But as I started to open the car door, John said, "Don't get out."

Thinking he was concerned that my big-city sensibilities weren't prepared for what would probably be a filthy bathroom, I said, "I'll be fine. I'll only be a minute."

I was halfway to the bathroom before I noticed a second sign that said WHITES ONLY. Desperate to go inside, I chose not to worry about it and was instead silently grateful that I wasn't black. Once I was inside, with the door shut behind me, it smelled so bad that I had to hold my breath. My shoes stuck to the floor as I stepped in dried urine. The seat was so disgusting that I didn't sit but instead stood over it, growing angrier and angrier at the entire situation. How could Leon expect me to move to this awful place? By the time I was finished, I was so mad that I took the Kleenex I'd used from my purse and threw it on the floor.

I couldn't tell the others what I had done—I was already embarrassed by my childish behavior—but I did tell them how revolting the restroom had been. "The sad thing," John said, "is that it'll be a black person who has to clean it." A wave of guilt washed over me as I thought of the dirty tissue I'd left on the floor. For the next hour, I stared out the window, my head beginning to ache as images raced through my mind. Mississippi. Shacks. Filthy restrooms. Mud. More mud.

TWO

❧

MOUND BAYOU

Largest U.S. Negro town; settled July 12, 1887, by ex-slaves of Joe Davis, who conceived idea before Civil War: Isaiah T. Montgomery (member of 1890 state convention) & his cousin, Benjamin T. Green.

—HISTORICAL MARKER PLACED AT THE TOWN BORDER ON HIGHWAY 61 BY THE MISSISSIPPI HISTORICAL COMMISSION IN 1951

An Hour Later

After driving south for another hour, we entered Mound Bayou, and Leon, pointing to a small side street, said, "That's where our house will be. And look over there. The town's got a brand-new swimming pool."

"How can they afford it?" I asked.

"They can't," he said, laughing. "You won't believe this, Aura, but the white folks in the next town paid for it."

"Why would they do that? I thought they hated everything about Mound Bayou."

His face grew animated as he shifted into his story-telling mode, his eyes sparkling and a playful grin spreading over his face. "They do. But they'd just put in a pool themselves, and one of their city council members raised a concern that with all the civil rights stuff going on, blacks might try to swim there."

"Did that happen?"

"No, but the rest of the council was so horrified at the thought that they offered to pay for a pool in Mound Bayou, in exchange for a promise that blacks would never try to swim in theirs."

At the crossroads, we left Highway 61, turned onto Township Road, and bounced over the railroad tracks. Moments later, when Leon pulled the car up in front of an attractive two-story house, it seemed out of place. Solidly constructed of red brick, it had an inviting front porch and an architectural style reminiscent of New England. Leon told me that this was the Montgomery House, built eighty years earlier by a former slave and now serving as a boardinghouse.

Leon led me up to the second floor, where half a dozen young men and women, some black, some white, met us. I tried to remember their names, but I had a headache and it was all I could do to figure out that they were somehow helping out with the clinic start-up. I must have appeared exhausted, for one of the women said, "You look like you could use a break. Why don't you lie down and get some rest?"

She showed me to a bed in the next room and placed a cool, damp cloth on my forehead. Breathing deeply, I let myself enjoy that special place between wakefulness and sleep as I listened to the murmur of Leon's voice quietly telling them about our drive down. The sound of one of them speaking angrily pulled me awake, however. "She crossed the line, Leon; she crossed the line."

"She had the gall to use a whites-only bathroom? How could she?" demanded one of the others, her voice cold with disgust. "It's hard enough having white folks move into town without her going and doing like that."

"Maybe she shouldn't come at all."

I inhaled sharply as I heard the fury in their voices. Then I buried my face in my pillow, all my anger about Leon's decision to move there washing over me in waves. Gradually, however, I succumbed to exhaustion and let myself start to drift off to sleep again. I heard Leon laughing, so the others must have gotten over their anger, which was a relief. I lost track for a while as I let sleep take over. Images flitted through my subconscious, first of antebellum mansions and then of the poor children playing by the shacks along Highway 61. Then, instead of the poor black children, it was my own children who were running about barefoot in the mud while my mother was hanging the laundry.

Then Leon appeared in my dream and grabbed my hand to dance. I kept trying to follow his steps, but the mud kept sucking at my feet and I couldn't move in time to the music. The music changed from the big bands that we'd listened to as teenagers to the melody of "Dixie," playing in the background like a movie soundtrack. I could feel my feet twitch as they tried to tap-dance to the tune, just as they'd been taught when I was a child. "Oh, I wish I was in the land of cotton. Old times there are not forgotten. Look away, look away, look away, Dixie Land."

As I felt myself waking up, I thought back to my dream and ruminated upon how the song had become an anthem to the Confederacy and the so-called glory of plantation life. Never again would I hear it without thinking of the shotgun shacks along Highway 61.

Suddenly, I realized what had awakened me. It was the smell of barbecued ribs. A powerful hunger drew me back to a room where the others were sitting on the floor, enjoying a late lunch. There I indulged in the tastiest, most succulent ribs I'd ever had. It was almost enough to make me forget how awful I felt about the conversation I'd overheard an hour earlier. Almost. Afraid that I'd inadvertently say something wrong, I ate my lunch in silence and listened as my husband and the others talked.

At first I tried to follow the conversation, but it rambled all over the place, covering topics I knew nothing about and people I'd never met. A few minutes of patiently pretending to pay attention in situations like this was expected of a physician's wife, but after an hour or so, my patience wore thin. This wasn't what I had traveled 1,500 miles to do. I wanted to see what the town was like, check out the schools, and see the plans for our new house, and we had less than twenty-four hours to accomplish all of that. Finally, when it appeared as if the meeting was drawing to an end without addressing any of our personal issues, I blurted out, "Wait! Can we talk about our house? I thought that—"

"What about it?" I recognized the voice of the woman who had responded so bitterly to the news of my using the whites-only bathroom. It didn't match her pleasant, youthful appearance. She couldn't have been more than twenty-five, barely older than my daughter. Dressed in blue jeans and a tie-dyed T-shirt, her long brown hair pulled back in a ponytail, she looked as if she'd be more at home on a college campus than here in this run-down house, strategizing about what was best for Mound Bayou.

I looked over at Leon and saw him shaking his head, his eyes begging me not to respond, but I couldn't keep quiet. "That little street on the way into town looks like a wonderful place for our home," I said in as placating a manner as I could muster, "but can anyone tell me anything about the construction schedule? We were hoping to move in before school starts in August. How can the house possibly be done by then when they haven't even broken ground?"

After an awkward silence, she said, "What do you need a new house for? You should live in a shack so you can understand what it's like."

"I can imagine how terrible—"

"No, you can't." She raised her voice and stood up as if to storm out of the room. "If people think you don't care about them, they won't come to the clinic, and they won't bring their children."

"I do care. Besides," I said coldly, "any parent with a

sick child will be grateful to have a doctor and won't care where we live."

"You're wro—"

"I'm not wrong. I'm guessing that you don't have any children yet, so you don't understand, but I know what I'm talking about. Right, Leon?"

Silence. I was on my own. "Look, I don't expect our home to be anything like what we have in Boston, but we do need indoor plumbing and electricity, and enough space for our three youngest children."

Finally, one of the others tried to calm me down by saying, "I'm sorry, Mrs. Kruger, but we really don't have any information about it."

"Then who does?"

No answer.

"Leon," I said, turning back to my husband, "we're running out of time. You told me we could see the house, but there's nothing there."

"I thought you'd be happy just to see the land."

"You mean you knew they hadn't started building?"

"Aura—"

"You knew? Don't you care?"

He just looked at me without saying a word, stunned that I'd interrupted him rather than let him calm me down, as I'd always done in the past. As I stared at him, waiting for an answer, it suddenly dawned on me: he didn't care.

For weeks the signs had been there, but I hadn't wanted to see them. Leon would have been perfectly content to live in this boardinghouse while I stayed behind in Massachusetts with the children. Although he still had a life and a medical practice in Boston, he was no longer satisfied with it. Every minute that he had been back there, he had been chomping at the bit to return to Mound Bayou to prepare for the clinic.

How different from our early days together! Then Leon told me about every aspect of his life, especially his dreams. Walking home from high school one day, he'd said, "When I step off the curb in Newton, it matters in China. We're all connected, and so what we do really matters. It's up to us to make the world a better place." I'd looked at him in a new light, appreciating that there was far more to this boy than the good-looking, popular dancer who was always joking around. Behind his extroverted persona was a deep thinker, someone who cared about the well-being of others.

That was all good and well when we were first falling in love. I'd even let myself get caught up in his enthusiasm when he spoke of saving the world, at least while we were sitting in the comfort of our own kitchen. But this was different. Real. The mud. The filthy bathroom. Worrying about the Ku Klux Klan following us down the highway. This wasn't a life that I had ever wanted, but Leon had decided that he did. I knew he loved the children and me and wanted us to be happy and safe, but somehow he'd lost track of that in his excitement about moving to Mound Bayou.

I was yanked back to the present when I realized that everyone else was standing up to leave.

"Wait a minute." They all stopped. "Please," I said, "can anyone tell me about the schools?"

Leon glared at me, shaking his head to tell me to be quiet. Ignoring him, I continued, "I'd really like to see them before we go."

The same woman who had been so hostile earlier said, "It's the weekend. They're closed."

"You can at least tell me about them."

One of the young men spoke up. "Okay, Mrs. Kruger," he said, "here's what we have. Mound Bayou has its own school district with an elementary school, a junior high, and JFK High."

One of the others jumped in. "There's also St. Gabriel's, which goes through eighth grade."

"A Catholic school?"

"More like a free mission school," he said, "just like the Catholic Church sponsors in poor countries." He went on to explain that the students were from all denominations. In fact, most of the children weren't Catholic but Southern Baptist. "Some folks seem to think that the teachers do a better job at St. Gabriel's than they do at the public school," he added. "And Father Guidry's very well respected in town."

The thought of sending my Jewish children to a Catholic school did not sit well with me. Despite that, I wanted my children at the best school available. So I asked if we could go by both the public and mission schools, even though it was the weekend and we wouldn't be able to go inside. After an awkward moment of silence, one of the young men offered to drive.

We crossed the railroad tracks to Highway 61 and headed through downtown, passing a perfectly maintained red brick post office with a freshly painted masonry front and a little cupola on the roof. Two elderly ladies stood chatting in front, dressed elegantly as if for church, even though it was Saturday. Then there were half a dozen shabby storefronts—a Laundromat, a tiny grocery store, a bar, a snack stand—one-story wooden buildings that looked like they'd seen better days. Across the street, in stark contrast, was a two-story brick building, the Bethel AME church.

Within moments the high school came into view, a brand-new building, its yellow bricks glistening in the sunlight. It was a one-story structure that might have appeared welcoming except for a bleakness resulting from a complete lack of trees. A line of small shrubs had been planted along the base of the front wall but hadn't yet had a chance to flourish.

After driving slowly by the high school, we did a U-turn and once again turned onto Township Road. On one side of the street were several homes, some brick, some wood. Although they were attractive and reasonably well maintained, they were tiny. They must have been well under a thousand square feet and couldn't have had space for more than two bedrooms, and small ones at that.

On the opposite side, the homes were little more than dilapidated shacks. The whole town was marked by these contrasts: a modern high school next door to the run-down hospital. A redbrick post office just down the street from a junkyard full of old cars. A brand-new swimming pool in a town with no other amenities.

St. Gabriel's was at the edge of town, just before the road turned to dirt. A cluster of four brick buildings—a rectory where the priest lived, the school itself, a convent for the nuns, and a church—it had an inviting feel to it. Behind the buildings was a field with a basketball court where a few young boys were shooting baskets.

A black man in his fifties or sixties, wearing a well-worn, earth-green sweater, was burning trash in a beaten-up metal can. Somewhere in the back of my mind it registered that there must not be any trash collection in town, and so the school janitor had to burn it.

Our guide approached the man and then gestured for Leon and me to come over. "Dr. and Mrs. Kruger, this is Father Guidry."

Hiding my surprise, I offered him my hand, which he took with both of his, smiling kindly. He had the kind of look that made me feel secure, as if he could see inside me and know what I was thinking, yet not judge me. His whole face beamed, his eyes crinkling up around the edges.

"Mrs. Kruger," he said, "you and your husband are doing a wonderful thing coming to Mound Bayou."

"We're looking forward to it," I answered glibly, my training since childhood allowing me to give a polite response even though it wasn't really true. His eyes held mine, and I could almost see him deciding whether to believe me.

"You must meet Sister Rosarita, our principal and eighth-grade teacher," he said as we walked slowly past the small brick church to the convent. His pride in the school was apparent as he described the facilities, the students, and the nuns with their junior-college education, sent by the Catholic Church of Cuba to help the poor people of the Mississippi Delta. "Most of our students can't afford to pay tuition. The lunch we serve them may be their only real meal of the day," said Father Guidry. "But not everybody is that badly off, and those who have money pay a few dollars a month for tuition to help offset our costs."

By this time, Sister Rosarita had joined us. Although a relatively short woman, she carried herself as if she were six feet tall, her back perfectly straight. The warm expression on her face did much to offset the severity of her attire—a traditional black habit that reached all the way down to her clunky, low-heeled black shoes. She opened the door to her eighth-grade classroom to reveal a neat, clean, and beautifully decorated refuge in the midst of the town's poverty. Every bulletin board was covered with colorful pictures and clippings from magazines. Although there weren't many of them, the bookshelves were well stocked.

"Tell me about your children, Mrs. Kruger. Do you have an eighth grader?" Her voice had a soft lilt to it, reflecting just a hint of a Spanish accent, and her grammar was textbook-perfect. That alone inclined me to enroll our children in her school.

"Actually, we do, Sister," I answered. "My older son, Philip, is fourteen."

"What's he like? What are his favorite subjects?"

"He likes all his classes, but his favorite is German. He plays the oboe in the school band and the guitar at home. And he loves being on the debate team." As my words describing Philip's accomplishments spilled out, it occurred to me that it might be coming across as boasting about our Newton schools in comparison with those of Mound Bayou. I could almost feel Leon tensing up in response, willing me to be more sensitive. Before I had a chance to amend my comments, however, Sister Rosarita responded.

"I'm afraid we don't offer any of that here at St. Gabriel's," she said apologetically, glancing at Father Guidry for support. "We're a small school and don't have many resources."

"What Sister means," Father Guidry added, "is that we have to focus on the basics. We'll give him a good background in reading and math."

"That's all right, Father Guidry," I hastened to say. "We understand."

But would Philip? I wasn't as worried about the two younger children; they weren't as involved in extracurricular activities and were too young to date, but Philip had an active social life that he'd be leaving behind. Would he ever forgive us for taking that away from him?

Sister Rosarita interrupted my thoughts by asking about our younger children.

"Charles will turn eleven this summer. He's very bright, but sometimes has a little trouble getting his schoolwork done."

Sister smiled warmly. "Our sixth- and seventh-grade teacher will be good for him. She has a special knack with boys like that."

"Then there's my youngest, Jo. She's nine and she's my little cricket, always into everything."

"Jo—that's an unusual name for a girl."

"It was Leon's idea. We named her after my favorite literary character—Jo, from *Little Women*," I added, not expecting her to recognize the title.

For the first time since we had arrived, I felt a warm glow when Sister said, "I'm familiar with the book, but it's been a long time since I read it. What was it about that character that made her your favorite?"

I don't know whether she was just being polite or was truly interested, or whether the natural teacher in her just had to ask. In any case, I answered her easily. "She was a loving mother, a compassionate teacher, and a nurturer—everything I wanted to be someday."

Sister nodded in encouragement.

"Then she created Plumfield, a boarding school that

was a sanctuary of learning and growth that I admired tremendously."

"We try to make St. Gabriel's a sanctuary like that. Now, tell me about your oldest. I hear that you'll be leaving behind a daughter in college. Is that true?"

I wondered how she knew about that. Then it suddenly dawned on me: the whole town had been talking about us, and everyone knew our business. I'd never lived in a small town before, but I'd heard that was what it was like. The lack of privacy might have bothered some people, but I didn't worry about it. I enjoyed having people pay attention to me. And, if I was honest about it, I liked being the center of attention.

Feeling a bit better, I answered Sister's question. "Yes. Connie is just finishing her freshman year at the University of Massachusetts. It's ironic. She picked a college close to home, yet here we are, planning to move fifteen hundred miles away. I know she can take care of herself and doesn't need to have us nearby, but it still feels wrong."

"I'm sure it's hard for you to leave her behind." My throat tightened at Sister's words, and I was afraid I'd break down. When Leon realized I wasn't going to respond, he glared at me and stepped in.

"She'll be fine," he said, abruptly putting an end to the conversation. I knew he believed that. He'd never worried about our children the way I did; he always found it easy to let them fend for themselves, to grow up on their own. It had never bothered me before, at least not very much. But now his attitude seemed based on a growing sense of indifference, rather than on an understanding that Connie was ready to be on her own.

Upset by this disheartening thought, I just wanted to get away from everybody. "Thank you so much, Sister Rosarita. I'm sure we'll be enrolling our children here at St. Gabriel's. But it's getting late and we'd better get going." Without giving Leon a chance to overrule me, I turned to walk back to the car.

Once there, I longed to tell him that I thought we were making a mistake and that it was too much to ask of our children, but he was so happy about being there that he would never have heard me. More than that, he didn't want to hear me. So I didn't try.

☙

BY THE TIME WE arrived at the Memphis airport the next morning, my anticipation of a first-class flight home chased away my sour mood. I'd never traveled in such luxury before and was looking forward to the experience, grateful to Leon's boss, Jack Geiger, for having spent the extra money for our return flight. It was a nice gesture, a little thank-you gift for the effort I'd put forth over the weekend.

John and Fleydra Hatch were already waiting at the departure gate. We joined them, vaguely aware of some curious stares as those around us took note of a black couple and a white couple chatting together. Leon excused himself to get our boarding passes, and when he returned, I glanced at the Hatches' documents to see if we were all in the same row.

"There must be some mistake," I said as I checked the location of their seats. "We're all supposed to be in first class."

"Don't worry. We'll be fine in coach," said John, shrugging his shoulders.

"You should go up to the counter and tell them to fix it," I replied without thinking, not understanding that their seat assignments were completely intentional; planes departing from Memphis did not seat black people in first class. John hesitated for a moment, clearly debating with himself whether to do as I suggested, but then he stood up and approached the gate agent.

"Excuse me, miss," he said, very softly. "I believe there's been a mistake. My wife and I have first-class tickets, but we were given seats in coach."

The woman hardly glanced at her paperwork before saying curtly, "First class is full." Shaking his head, John returned to our seats, taking Fleydra's hand as he sat down.

Slowly, I realized exactly what had happened, that no mistake had been made. "They can't do this to you, John," I said. "You should go back up to the desk and demand—"

"Aura, it's not worth the fight," he answered.

Suddenly, all the times when I'd seen discrimination in the past flashed through my mind: My father excluded from golf clubs because we were Jewish. Schoolmates calling me "Christ Killer" and refusing to play with me during the week before Easter. The other army wives shunning me for the same reason. And—as I was so freshly aware—the whites-only restroom on the way to Mound Bayou. Anger welled up inside me, and I spat out, "Jack spent the money for first-class tickets. They have no right to take that away from you."

Leon put a hand on my arm. Tired of being treated like a naive child, I pulled away. "Leon, if John won't do it, then you should. They won't turn *you* down." When he didn't get up, I started to stand, saying, "If you won't go straighten this out, then I will."

Leon stopped me. "I'll do it," he mumbled with a scowl, taking the tickets and boarding passes up to the agent. Then, acting as if the tickets were ours, he requested that she give him first-class seats.

"No problem, sir. We can fix that for you right away." Within moments, she handed Leon the new paperwork.

≈

WAITING ON THE TARMAC for takeoff, I felt a familiar tightening in the pit of my stomach as I thought about the dangers of air travel, a fear that I'd had to contend with since World War II, when several of Leon's and my friends were killed in training accidents. As he'd always done in the past, Leon reached for my hand to comfort me. But for the first time since we'd started dating as teenagers, I pulled my hand away. Since he'd offered so little support throughout the weekend, I didn't want it now.

THREE

❦

LIVING *with* DON QUIXOTE

To attain the impossible, one must attempt the absurd.

—MIGUEL DE CERVANTES SAAVEDRA

Five Weeks Earlier
Newton, Massachusetts — February 1967

The last notes of Beethoven's Ninth Symphony faded away as I stood at the stove in my high heels, stirring a pot of Campbell's tomato soup with rice and waiting for Leon and our two younger children to come home for lunch. I'd spent the morning running errands and straightening the house and was looking forward to sharing the next hour with my family.

The front door slammed. "Mom, we're home!" Jo called. "What's for lunch?" shouted Charles. Pausing just long enough to tear off their boots and jackets before dashing for the kitchen, they stopped for hugs on their way to the table, already chattering away about their morning.

"My class went to the library," Charles began, "and—"

"Mine too," said Jo, "and I found a book about horseback riding in the mountains." This was her latest phase. She was reading everything she could find about life in the Southwest. She never played house like most other nine-year-old girls. She played at being a cowboy or a superhero.

"I got a book about Mozart," Charles said, continuing where he'd left off. He was my pianist, spending hours a day at the keyboard, oblivious to the rest of the household. Although only ten, he dreamed of someday performing in Carnegie Hall. Somehow, his physical clumsiness disappeared the moment he sat at the piano, his fingers flying over the keys so fast that you could barely see them. That may have been the only time he was completely happy, unmindful of his difficulties in school and the constant pressure from his father to be neater and better organized.

Charles stopped talking as soon as I placed his soup in front of him. It was his favorite lunch, and I tried to make it often, despite the fact that it annoyed his father to watch him pick out pieces of rice with his fingers. As I started toward the stove to dish out a bowl for Jo, I heard Leon coming in. He was usually able to join us for lunch because his pediatrics office was right next to the house. He could go out the back door of the office, walk across our backyard, and climb the stairs to the screened-in porch where the whole neighborhood gathered each year to celebrate the start of summer with a giant barbecue.

On this particular day, however, I hadn't been sure he'd make it home on time. He'd had a meeting in South Boston with two doctors from Tufts University about working at a clinic they'd built at the Columbia Point housing project. When I reached out to hug him hello, he instead grabbed my hand and spun me about the kitchen, singing, "You are my sunshine, my only sunshine. You make me happy when skies are gray . . ."

Our miniature French poodle, Pepper, started barking and jumping up on the two of us. Leon ended our dance with a dip and a kiss. Pulling out my chair, he said, "You sit down, Aura. I'll get the soup."

As he walked over to the stove, I could hear my mother telling me how lucky I was to have a husband who didn't mind helping around the house. When Leon returned to the table, he sat in the chair next to me, always preferring to sit there rather than at the head of the table.

"If you could live anywhere in the world," he said, brandishing his spoon, "where would it be?"

Without missing a beat, Jo said, "Arizona. Then I could have a horse and we could explore the desert and the mountains and caves, and maybe we'd even find some old Indian artifacts . . ." My little tomboy was an odd mix, splitting her time between playing games with the neighborhood children and reading for hours on end. As she chattered away, she reminded me of Dickens's *The Cricket on the Hearth*, and I knew that were she standing up, she'd be bouncing from one foot to the other. Finally, when she paused for a breath, Charles said, "Hawaii!"

He loved our summers on Cape Cod with my parents and my sister's family. Somewhat of a loner during the school year, he cherished the ready-made companionship of seven cousins and three siblings all under one roof. For years he'd talked about someday going to Hawaii, figuring that if Cape Cod was good, an island in the middle of the Pacific would be even better.

I had a different island in mind. Leon and I had recently returned from celebrating our twenty-fifth wedding anniversary in Puerto Rico, and I could still taste the sweet mango punch. I pictured my handsome husband standing in the sand by our towels, ready for a quick swim in the pounding surf. He had retained his youthful features and still looked basically the same as he had when I first knew him, in high school. Back then, all the girls had swooned over him, saying he was the "smoothest." And even after he declared his love for me, I never quite got over thinking that I didn't deserve him. Unusually short, with dark hair and a flat chest, I was a far cry from the busty, leggy blondes who were so popular in the movies of the day.

"It's your turn, Aura," Leon said with a smile, pulling me back to the present. "Where would you like to live?"

"Puerto Rico," I said.

"You're all wrong," he said, his voice rising in excitement. "We're going to *Mississippi*."

I started to speak, but initially no words came out. After a moment, I managed to stutter, "M-Mississippi?"

"Yes," he answered, so enthusiastic that he failed to notice that I wasn't sharing his enthusiasm. "Pack up the house and call a real estate agent."

"Leon, we can't move now. What about school?"

"I know, I know. Don't worry. You and the children can stay here until June. I'll commute."

"Why do we have to wait?" asked Jo.

Noticing my hands shaking as the questions tumbled through my head, I knew that Leon and I needed to have a serious conversation, one that we shouldn't conduct in front of the children. So I stood up from the table and said, "Time to go back to school."

Charles followed me to the front hall, all the time trying to talk me into letting them stay. "Can't we just stay for a few minutes? We can be late. I want to hear about the move. Our teachers won't mind—"

"No," I answered, cutting him off as I helped him put on his boots and coat, grateful that Jo was taking care of herself. "We'll tell you all about it tonight over dinner."

Then I waved good-bye and closed the door behind them. I paused for a moment with my hand on the knob and my head leaning against the door, trying to regain my composure, before returning to the table.

"All right, Leon. Tell me everything that happened."

"It was amazing, Aura, just amazing. When I spoke with Jack Geiger and Count Gibson about helping out at the Columbia Point clinic here in Boston, they told me they're building another clinic in Mississippi, in the poorest spot in the country."

"And they want you to work at that one instead?"

Jumping up, he began pacing about the kitchen. "They don't just want me to *work* there, Aura. They want me to be the medical director. Can you believe it? Mound Bayou is this tiny, all-black town."

"What do you mean, 'all black'?"

"It's been that way since just after the Civil War. With the exception of a few other people moving down with the project, we'll be the only white people."

I felt the blood rushing to my head as his words sank in. I'd supported his decision two years earlier to return to school to get a degree in public health so that he could expand beyond his pediatric practice. I'd accompanied him to a United Nations recruiting session while he looked into serving on the SS *Hope* as it brought medical care to the developing world. But never had I imagined that my support would include uprooting our family and following him to the Deep South.

"So if you take the job, we'd move there for a few months?"

"There's no *if*, Aura," he said, sitting next to me again. "They offered me the job, and I accepted."

"You accepted?"

"Yes. And they gave me a two-year contract."

Stunned, I couldn't say a word. Leon, too excited to notice that I was upset, blithely stood up to leave. "I've got patients waiting," he said. "We'll talk more tonight."

With that, he walked toward the back door. Then he stopped and turned toward me. I let myself hope that he was going to ask my opinion about his decision, or at least thank me for understanding. Instead, all he said was "Don't forget to call a real estate agent."

"Leon—"

"No time now. I'm already late for my next appointment." Then he dashed out, leaving me in a state of shock.

For several minutes, I sat staring at the wall. My stomach was so tense that the bowl of soup I'd just consumed felt like a ton of bricks. When I began to feel lightheaded, I realized that I'd been holding my breath and willed myself to exhale.

In our twenty-five years of marriage, Leon and I had dealt with more than our fair share of crises, and we'd always managed because we were partners. I had seen him through pilot training during World War II and supported him through medical school. He'd encouraged me to work outside the home and challenge myself. When we were told we could never have children, we'd decided together to pursue adoption and artificial insemination. Together we had figured out a way to create the family we both wanted. But this time, it was as if my desires didn't matter. My Don Quixote was out to save the world, whether or not I was there by his side.

I understood that Leon wanted to make a difference. What I couldn't understand was why he was dissatisfied with the life we'd built for ourselves there in Newton, why he couldn't battle his windmills from there. By all outward measures, we should have been the happiest couple on Earth. We lived in a vibrant community with close friends for us and top-rated schools for our children.

His pediatric practice was flourishing, and for the first time since med school, we were financially secure.

As I looked about the kitchen now, I let the memories flow. I could still see the ketchup stain on the ceiling from the day the children staged a contest to see who could squirt the highest. I remembered the first time my oldest child, Connie, made a cake and turned the oven to BROIL instead of BAKE; it was all I could do to let her discover her mistake on her own rather than rescue her.

I wandered into the dining room and felt a warm glow as I looked at the huge antique table at which we'd hosted countless Thanksgiving dinners for my parents and my sister and her seven children. For a moment, I could picture them all gathered together, laughing and eating turkey. Then it was as if I saw their laughter die away as they all began to wave good-bye, their smiles growing somber as they realized this would be our last Thanksgiving together—as I realized that this part of my life was over.

In a daze, I walked to the window and stared out over the front yard, which had served as a football field, a baseball diamond, and, in winter, a snow fort. I pictured our children running about with their friends, giggling as they played tag. My knees felt weak as I remembered a day not so long ago when Leon and I had stood on the porch, looked into the yard, and counted over a dozen children rushing about. He'd hugged me and said, "Isn't it wonderful that you now have what you've always wanted?" I'd agreed with him immediately, for our life together was indeed truly wonderful. It hadn't occurred to me at the time that he'd commented on what *I* had wanted, not what *we* had wanted together.

I glanced up the stairs and saw myself almost a dozen years earlier, struggling to stay upright as I held toddler Philip in one arm, baby Charles in the other, and unborn Jo in my belly. Now Connie was at college, Philip's voice had changed, and I could no longer call Charles and Jo my little bear cubs, for it had been years since they had wrestled together on the floor for hours on end.

Without even realizing that I had climbed the stairs, I found myself sitting on our great big bed, thinking about our Sunday evenings with our four children, our dog, and our cat all sprawled there together, watching *The Ed Sullivan Show* on our little black-and-white television. For close to a year, Leon's teenage niece Susan had joined us as well.

One day, after Susan had been living with us for a few months, she said, "Auntie Aura, I know you believe in being honest with the children. Why do you lie to them about money?"

Confused, I said, "What do you mean, darling?"

"I heard you tell Charles and Jo that you're rich."

"But, sweetie, we *are* rich. We have a beautiful home in a nice neighborhood and food on our table every day. We're better off than ninety percent of the world's population."

Her answer made me laugh. "Then why do my parents always refer to you as 'the poor relations'?"

Compared with her parents, we were indeed poor. Until recently, we'd had no extra funds for vacations, and our children often had only two sets of clothes, one on their backs and one in the laundry. But we had everything we needed, and we were happy with what we had. At least I was. But was Leon? Thoughts of the bombshell he'd dropped over lunch interrupted my reminiscing, and once again I struggled to understand what had happened, how he could possibly want to uproot our family and move to the middle of nowhere.

I didn't struggle for long, however. In my typical Pollyanna style, I instead buried the struggle and forced myself to think positively. I could hear my grandma Lena reprimanding me for complaining about having to drag eight pails of garbage up to the street each week. Since we'd never hired a janitor to help out at Leon's office, I took care of the medical garbage as well as our family's, and she'd say, with her slightly Yiddish inflection, "Aura, you should be happy that you're well enough and strong enough to do it. Not everybody is. And don't pout at me. That sour look will freeze on your face."

Growing up with her optimistic influence, I'd internalized her philosophy. One time, when I was talking with Leon's brother, Everett, about religion, he said, "Aura, why do you believe in God? I know some people do because they need to pray whenever they want something. But you never ask for anything."

"I need God so I can thank Him."

Returning to the kitchen, still numb from the news of Leon's decision to move, I reminded myself that despite this newest challenge, I still had much to be thankful for. Leon was a good man who cared about others, and— although I feared it might take more strength than I possessed—I vowed to at least try to be the trouper Leon expected me to be. More than that, it was what the children needed me to be. They should never know how upset I was at the prospect of moving to Mississippi, how it broke my heart to contemplate leaving behind our family and friends.

Mississippi. The Deep South. The last time I had been there, Leon had been a pilot in training during World War II and had been sent to a base in South Carolina. I joined him shortly after he was transferred, and I settled into a rented room in a house near the airfield. After waiting what seemed like forever before Leon obtained permission for me to visit, I caught a bus to the camp, eager for our reunion after two months apart. When I arrived, we embraced like newlyweds, which we practically still were, and I couldn't get enough of looking at him and listening to his stories about learning to fly.

But when we sat down in the mess hall to have dinner with a couple of his army buddies, my mood plummeted and I lost my appetite. There were gnats everywhere, even crawling around in the whites of Leon's and his friends' eyes. Feeling sick to my stomach, I realized that they must be in *my* eyes as well. The others seemed not to notice, however, so, despite my disgust, I picked up my fork and tried to force myself to eat. I couldn't. It was impossible to take a bite without eating gnats as well.

When I said something, Leon reprimanded me, saying, "You're behaving like a spoiled little girl. If you can't deal with the conditions, maybe you should go back to Boston and live with your parents."

Although I felt distraught and embarrassed, I knew Leon was right in that there was nothing to do but accept the gnats. Nobody else seemed to mind them, so why should I? Was I really as spoiled as he accused me of being? I appreciated that Leon challenged me to be more tolerant of difficult situations, but did he have to speak to me like a child, especially in front of his friends? Not knowing what else to do, I swallowed my hurt, along with the gnats, and promised myself I would be better in the future and make Leon proud of me, rather than ashamed.

I didn't complain. In our twenty-five years of marriage, I never complained, even when I felt as if Leon was being unfair. Despite my best efforts, I couldn't tell him when I was upset. My mouth went dry and my throat tightened up. If I attempted to say anything, I started to cry. So I didn't try. Sometimes he tried to figure out what was bothering me; most of the time, though, he just waited for me to regain my composure.

I appreciated his patience. He was much gentler than my father had been. Daddy was strict and expected me to do exactly as he said, no questions asked. I knew he loved me, but he ordered me about, sometimes making me feel like one of his runners. Those were the men who handled the money for the numbers racket that my father operated as part of the Jewish Mafia.

As a child, I lived in fear that my friends would ask what my father did for a living, and I longed for the day he would go into a legitimate business, as he so often promised. I found it especially frustrating during my long talks with Leon while walking home from high school. I ached to share that aspect of my life with him but was afraid to do so, both because I worried about my father's safety if people found out about him and because I didn't want Leon to lose respect for me and stop being my friend. It made me love him that much more when he learned the truth shortly after we were married and he never held it against me.

He'd stood by me then, and now it was my turn to

stand by him. I couldn't tell him that it broke my heart to contemplate leaving behind our family and friends to move to Mississippi. I couldn't. I considered, ever so briefly, the possibility of suggesting that Leon go to Mound Bayou without us. My sister's husband worked in Washington, DC, while the family lived in Connecticut, and they managed well enough. But that wasn't the kind of marriage I wanted.

It wasn't just that. I was afraid that if Leon left for Mississippi on his own, I might never see him again. At first he'd travel back and forth to see us each month, but then he'd get caught up in the work and go longer and longer between visits. I couldn't let that happen. I didn't dare force him to make a choice between his career and his family. Sadly, I knew the children and I would lose.

⁂

I PICKED UP THE phone on the kitchen counter and called our friend and neighbor Mary Louise O'Malley, who happened to be a real estate agent.

"We need you to sell the house for us," I told her.

"You're moving? When? Where?"

For a moment, my voice caught in my throat; then I managed to say, "Mississippi," as I squeezed my eyes shut and felt the tears begin to flow. I forced myself to continue. "Leon's been asked to be the medical director for a new clinic there."

"But what about you, dear? Your life is here."

"You know me, Mary Louise. I loved traveling around the country with Leon during his Army Air Corps training . . ." My voice trailed off as I tried to think of something positive to add.

"Whom are you trying to convince, Aura, me or you?"

"Oh, there's no question it'll be difficult. We'll be in a very poor town, and we'll be one of only a few white families—"

"You'll what?"

"It's an all-black town."

"You can't be serious about this, Aura," she said, her voice rising in disbelief. "It won't be safe. What about the children?"

"Oh, they'll be okay," I said, silently sharing Mary Louise's concern but willing myself to believe that Leon would never knowingly put our family in harm's way. With that, I told her we wanted to sell the place by the end of the school year.

Then I hung up the phone, laid my head down on the table, and cried, with nobody to hear but the dog and the cat.

—THURGOOD MARSHALL, CIVIL RIGHTS LAWYER AND FIRST
   BLACK SUPREME COURT JUSTICE, SPEAKING TO THE
   AMERICAN BAR ASSOCIATION IN 1988

FOUR

THE LAND of COTTON

A child born to a Black mother in a state like Mississippi … has exactly the same rights as a white baby born to the wealthiest person in the United States. It's not true, but I challenge anyone to say it is not a goal worth working for.

—THURGOOD MARSHALL, CIVIL RIGHTS LAWYER AND FIRST BLACK SUPREME COURT JUSTICE, SPEAKING TO THE AMERICAN BAR ASSOCIATION IN 1988

Summer 1967

O ur life in Newton somehow seemed unreal after that
first trip to Mississippi. I went through the motions
—attending school functions, listening to the children talk
about their friends—but my heart wasn't in it. What was
the point of it all, when everything was going to change
so abruptly as soon as the school year drew to a close and
our new house was completed? Then we'd drive away one
last time, perhaps never to return.

Throughout it all, I was deeply disturbed that construction hadn't even started. I had visions of living in a
motel or, even worse, of staying with my parents in New
England while Leon moved to Mound Bayou. Each
evening over dinner, I waited for him to tell me that work
had begun.

After what seemed like an eternity, Leon finally came
home one day and said that his boss was sending us back
to Mississippi—this time to the state capital—so we could
sign papers for the house.

When we arrived in Jackson, we got a very different
view of Mississippi than we had the time before. Though
not a large city, Jackson was considerably bigger than any
of the towns through which we'd driven en route to
Mound Bayou. There were restaurants, museums, even a
few colleges. Saying that we had some time to kill before
our meeting with the lawyer, Leon suggested that we drive
around a bit and explore. We passed a big, white clapboard
house that wouldn't have looked the least out of place in
Boston. A few minutes later we drove by the governor's

residence, with its two-story-high columns reminiscent of the old South. "See that art deco–style building, the one with the blue panels?" Leon asked. "That's the Greyhound bus station, where the Freedom Riders ended up back in 1961."

"It's like seeing a bit of history," I answered, thinking how different this history was from what I'd grown up with living in New England.

"It is," he agreed. "Just a little way from here is Tougaloo College, an all-black college. Their students were in the newspapers a while back because some of them tried to hold a 'read-in' at the public library and got kicked out because it was whites only. You can see the story of the civil rights movement everywhere you look."

My history lesson ended when we ran out of time and had to head for the lawyer. I looked forward to seeing the drawings for our new home, but when we arrived, the lawyer said, "I'm sorry to have to tell you this, Mrs. Kruger, but there are no construction plans."

"How can we sign a contract if we don't have any plans?"

"Contract?"

"Yes, contract," I said. "That's why we're here: to sign a contract so we can begin building. We're already late getting started."

"I'm afraid there's been some sort of misunderstanding, ma'am. I don't have any contract for you."

"Then why are we here?" I looked to Leon to see if he had any answers, but he looked just as lost as I felt.

"This is just a chance for us to get to know each other, since we'll probably be working together in the future, once things settle down."

"But—"

"I'm sorry, Mrs. Kruger. I wish I could help you. But I can't just pull plans and a contract out of the air."

I couldn't answer.

"Don't worry, Aura," Leon said, trying to comfort me. "We'll get this straightened out. I'll figure it out when we get back home."

Silently I followed him out the door, too stunned to say a word. Why had Jack sent us here if it wasn't to sign papers? Was there supposed to have been a contract waiting for us that had just fallen through at the last minute? Had Jack Geiger known all along that we still had no contract but figured a weekend vacation in Jackson would make up for that? Had Leon been in on the pretense?

Once we were back in the car, Leon tried to calm me by driving around again, showing me some of the more prosperous neighborhoods of Jackson. They were beautiful, but served only as a reminder that we were selling my home in Boston and still had no home in Mississippi. Leon, however, as he always did, understood my sour mood and did what he could to pull me out of it by telling me about the Jewish community in Jackson.

"I didn't know there were any Jews in Mississippi," I said, my interest in the conversation helping me to recover from the meeting with the lawyer. I was delighted to know that we wouldn't be the only Jews in our new state, but I was dismayed when Leon told me that earlier that week, the Ku Klux Klan had blown up a temple in Jackson.

⁂

THE TENSION BETWEEN LEON and me grew as mid-June turned to late June and we still had no home in Mound Bayou. The children finished up at school, and Leon shut down his pediatrics practice. I started giving away our possessions, knowing that our future housing—whatever it might be—would be significantly smaller than the ten rooms we had in Newton. Helping Jo pack up her belongings, I cringed inside as I explained that in Mound Bayou, there wouldn't be space for everything.

"That's okay, Mom. I don't mind."

Jo was my easy child, resilient and willing to try anything. She really meant it when she said she didn't care. I noticed the journal I'd given her still sitting on her desk. She followed my eyes and said, "Is it okay if I don't pack my diary in the boxes? I want to write in it over the summer." I hugged her as I told her that would be fine.

"I've already been using it," she said. "Do you want to know what I'm writing about?"

I nodded.

"I'm trying to figure out what black people are like so I'll be ready when we get to Mississippi."

I wanted to tell her that black people were just like us, but something in her innocent curiosity kept me from interrupting.

"There's one black girl in my class, and I wrote about her."

Unaware that Jo had a black friend, I asked her to tell me more about Naomi.

"We'd never really been friends before. She kind of scared me because she never smiles. But I started hanging out with her at recess, and now she doesn't seem any different from the other kids."

"That's a good point," I said, wanting to ask if I could see what she wrote but resisting the temptation, since I'd promised that she could keep her diary private.

"So then I asked Mrs. Johnson what Mound Bayou would be like."

Mrs. Johnson was the lady who helped me with the housecleaning once a week. She always set up the ironing board in Jo's bedroom and was usually there when Jo came home from school. I knew the two of them talked, but I never listened in.

"What did she tell you?"

"She said, 'Child, why would I know anything about Mound Bayou?'"

I was impressed with how well Jo was able to imitate Mrs. Johnson's manner of speaking. "Did she say anything else?"

"When I told her she should know because she was black, she said, 'I ain't never been outside of Boston, honey. You'll have to be asking somebody else.' Then she said that I should say she was Negro, not black. Why is that?"

"It's because she's older. In her generation, the word 'Negro' was an improvement over what was used in the past. But now the young people want to be called black."

❧

WHILE WE WERE BUSY PACKING, Leon's patients organized a farewell party for him. At the banquet, one person after another stood up to thank Leon for his care and concern over the years, praising every aspect of his work. On the way home, Leon said, "If I had realized how my patients felt, I might not have wanted to leave!"

"How can you say that? Your patients have always loved you."

"I suppose. But tonight seemed different, somehow. They made me feel special, appreciated."

"And if you'd realized this before, you would have been happy to stay?"

No answer.

"Leon?"

Silence. My jaw clenched as I allowed myself a brief moment of wishing for what might have been. I hated not knowing where we would live, what kind of home we would have. But I wouldn't tell anyone how I felt.

The consummate actress, I convinced everyone that I bought into Leon's dream of serving humanity by moving to Mound Bayou and believed it to be the best thing for the family. At least, I thought so at the time. Years later, Charles told me he saw right through my pretense and referred to it as "the great lie." He said, "The lie was that it was all good—we were a wonderful family and it was a big adventure and nothing was being taken away from us and we were all going to write wonderful books and be famous and we were important and fabulous and everybody would love us and think we were the greatest thing since sliced bread." He couldn't say anything at the time, though; he thought that because I refused to see anything but the good, he wasn't allowed to notice the bad. And he was alone in his misery.

❧

WE LEFT OUR HOME in Newton and moved in with my parents on Cape Cod. By now the move to Mississippi was only a month away, and still we had no housing. Jack Geiger suggested that Leon go on his own and leave the family behind; the children and I would continue to live with my folks.

I didn't want that. I wanted to be with my husband

and keep our family together. I was thus relieved when Leon came home one day and said that Jack had called a meeting to go over our housing options. As we drove to Boston from the Cape, my mood lifted. Everything was going to be okay.

When we arrived, Jack joked, "I know you're concerned about your house. But don't worry. At least the weather is warm. If you have to use an outhouse, you won't freeze." Then he tried to end the meeting before telling us where we would live, but I refused to get up. "If I have to, I'll dump my piano on the main street of town and set up housekeeping there," I told him. Jack agreed to bring in trailers.

After that, I tried to be content. Summers on Cape Cod with my parents had always soothed me, reenergizing me for whatever happened next. And for a while, this summer seemed no different. We went swimming every day at Craigville Beach, and afterward we'd head for the Four Seas restaurant for ice-cream cones. One night, I woke up at about two in the morning and sat on my bed, looking out the open window. The pine trees stood out in the moonlight, rustling in the gentle breeze. Taking a deep breath, I could smell their sweet scent. But then the deep breath turned to a sigh as I let the feelings of hopelessness and helplessness wash over me. My beautiful home in Newton was gone, and I would be moving to a strange town where I'd know not a soul and would live in a trailer. In three short weeks, July would turn to August and we'd be in Mississippi.

Although I was happy to be on our way when it was time to go, I found it difficult saying good-bye to Connie and my parents, as I knew it would be many months before

I'd see them again. I kept watching them through the back window of the car, waving and treasuring the sight of the three of them waving back.

Forcing myself to remain composed, I joined the children in talking about our upcoming adventure. Leon and I had decided to make the trip a real vacation by taking time to see the country and enjoy ourselves. We began our sightseeing in New York City, where we took a boat ride around Staten Island and saw the Statue of Liberty. In Washington, DC, we stopped to walk up the steps of the Lincoln Memorial. In Virginia, we explored the Blue Ridge Mountains and the Shenandoah Valley. Each day we rose before dawn and drove for an hour before stopping for breakfast. Everyone was in high spirits, enjoying both the sightseeing and one another's company.

Once we arrived in Mississippi, we moved into a Holiday Inn Jr.—a smaller, less luxurious version of the large hotel chain. When we'd first arrived in Cleveland, we had driven by another motel en route to ours. It had a swimming pool in front, with a long, curvy slide.

"Will our motel have a pool like that?" asked Charles.

"With a slide?" added Jo.

"No," I answered, knowing they'd be disappointed.

"Why can't we stay here, then?" Philip asked, obviously feeling a bit cheated.

"There are two reasons. First, it costs more, and we have to save our money. But more importantly, that pool is for whites only, and we don't want to support a segregated motel."

As soon as I explained, the children accepted our decision. I'd never told them about my awful experience using the whites-only bathroom on my first trip to Mound Bayou and how I'd gotten everyone so angry with me, but they already understood the importance of our taking a stand against discrimination.

༄

IT WAS STILL DARK out when my portable alarm clock went off at six in the morning. Leon was already up and getting dressed. I stepped through the connecting door to Jo's room and shook her awake, then walked across the hall to knock on the doors of the boys' rooms. We wanted to be at the motel restaurant by six thirty, when it opened.

Pancakes on a school day! The children were visibly pleased with the arrangement, perfectly content with hotel living. They busily filled in the state names on the map outlined on our paper place mats, challenging each other to remember all the midwestern states, which had such similar shapes.

As Leon signed the check, I suggested that we gather in front of the hotel sign to take our traditional first-day-of-school pictures. He said, "No time. I've got to drop the kids off early to get to a meeting. We can get pictures in front of the trailers in a few weeks."

Sadly, it occurred to me that this was only one of many traditions we would forgo in Mississippi. My parents had taken pictures of my sister and me every year on the first day of school, and I'd continued the pattern with my own children. I knew that Leon was right, that we could easily pull out the camera another morning. Nevertheless, as I waved good-bye and watched my children depart for their first day in Mound Bayou, I felt my mood plummet.

Sitting alone in the motel a few minutes later, I tried to read. My eyes followed the words, but my mind was with the children. What would their first day be like? Would they make friends? Would their black classmates accept them? They had all been bubbling over during breakfast, not the least bit concerned, but would they still feel the same after their first day? I ached to be with them, to walk them into their classrooms and say a proper good-bye, but that would have meant that Leon would have had to drive me the twenty minutes back to Cleveland. He couldn't make the time.

THE DAYS TOOK ON a pleasant rhythm. After breakfast each morning, Leon drove the children to school and then spent the day in Mound Bayou, working in the community, preparing to open up the clinic in its initial, temporary quarters in a five-room church parsonage. I passed the time much as I had when I'd followed Leon around the country during World War II—reading, doing needlework, and writing letters. For the first time in years, I felt completely rested.

Occasionally I would look out the window of my tiny motel room, staring at the wasteland around me, feeling lost and lonely. Fortunately, those moments passed quickly, and most of the time I was pleased with how well the children were adjusting to their new life.

Because we took all our meals at the motel restaurant, I didn't have to worry about grocery shopping and cooking. All that was left for me to do was laundry. Twice a week, I gathered up our dirty clothes and took them to the Laundromat in Mound Bayou. It would have been easier to wash our clothes in Cleveland, but Leon told me that it was important to make the extra effort. He wanted to demonstrate not only that we were supporting the Mound Bayou economy but also that we had no problem using a washer and dryer previously used by black people, something the white people of Cleveland would generally not do. So I sat by myself, barely able to read by the dim light, ignored by the other women there and not letting myself reach out to them for fear of saying something wrong.

When our trailers arrived a couple of weeks later, we set them up on a vacant lot we'd purchased, a few blocks away from the lot I'd been shown on that first trip to Mound Bayou several months earlier. That one hadn't worked out because we'd wanted to buy the land and that owner would only rent to us. Obtaining property was more difficult than we'd imagined. At first, some of the townspeople, fearful of what could happen if white people got an economic foothold in town, didn't want anyone to sell us land. When we promised to sell it back to someone in the black community when it was time for us to leave, however, we were able to find a seller. The lot was perfect: centrally located on one of the few paved streets, two blocks from the junior and senior high schools in one direction, and two doors down from the Catholic school in the other.

Leon and I had decided on two trailers so that the children could each have their own bedroom. Their rooms were tiny—with barely enough space for a twin bed, a small desk, and an even smaller bureau—but at least there would be no arguments about sharing space. Combined, the two trailers were about 1,200 square feet—less than a fourth of what we'd had in Boston. But they had indoor plumbing.

The trailers were made of white metal, with black shutters around the windows. The larger one was sixty feet long and had a bedroom at each end, as well as a bathroom, kitchen, dining room, and laundry room. Leon and I took the bedroom closest to the street and gave the back one to Jo. The smaller trailer—which we placed parallel to the first and about twelve feet away—was forty feet long and also had a bedroom at each end. Between the bedrooms were a living room and bathroom. The two boys stayed in this trailer; thirteen-year-old Philip was thrilled with his independence, but eleven-year-old Charles found it disconcerting to be so far away from his parents.

In some ways, I truly liked our trailers. I had air-conditioning for the first time in my life, and everything was new. We were able to fit much of the living and dining room furniture from our old house and to make the trailers feel like home. Despite that, I was miserable with the setup, for it left me separated from the boys. I couldn't sleep for the first few nights after we moved in. I felt sick to my stomach and stood staring out my bedroom window at the other trailer, wishing we were back in our old house. I knew it wasn't logical, but I worried that a tornado would come and blow away the smaller trailer. What was entirely rational, on the other hand, was how sad I was that Charles felt I'd deserted him. What made me feel even worse was the recognition that maybe I had. If he was sick during the night, I couldn't hear him call out. If he had a bad dream—as he so often did—he couldn't walk down the hall to our bedroom to seek comfort. I was distraught.

Leon understood my concern and suggested that we

hire a carpenter to build a connecting room, creating in the process a storage area and new front and back doors. An added bonus was that it made the trailers look and feel more like a house. It was a marked improvement, and the boys no longer had to walk outside through the rain and mud to reach us from their bedrooms.

The yard, completely bare, was another story. In back, the dirt stretched for all of ten feet before opening up onto a huge field overgrown with weeds. I hoped that eventually we might plant some shrubs or small trees around the trailers so the yard wouldn't look so bleak.

This wasn't the first time our yard had looked barren. In Newton, we'd never had time or money for landscaping. As happy as Leon and I were when we looked out over our yard, my mother saw scrawny grass and large patches of dirt. After several weeks of telling us we should do something about it, she took matters into her own hands and—unbeknownst to me—called the gardener she'd used for thirty years.

Answering the doorbell one afternoon, I was surprised to see him standing there. He said, "Aura, remember me? I was—"

"Mr. Cedrone!" I exclaimed. "Of course I remember you. How are your children? I've never forgotten how much I loved to play with them when I was a little girl."

For a long time, we stood on the front porch, watching seven or eight children chasing each other about in a game of tag. Finally, he said, "Aura, grow children now, grass later."

His words came back to me as I looked out from our ramshackle trailers held together by a makeshift porch. It was still home. There was barely room to walk around the old dining table we'd brought from Boston, but at least we'd made space in the living room for our studio upright piano, and we'd even found someone in town to tune it for us and to give Charles lessons. Mound Bayou wasn't quite the cultural wasteland I'd feared it would be.

August 1967

Our first Friday night in the trailers, the JFK High School Mighty Hornets were facing the football team from the all-black high school in Shelby, eight miles to the north. All of Mound Bayou was heading to the field for the first home game of the season, as if in a parade. Some families carried picnic baskets containing their dinners; others carried babies too young to walk.

And it wasn't just the townspeople. Fans came from miles away, greatly anticipating their entertainment on this hot, sultry evening. Township Road was lined with dusty old pickup trucks from the nearby towns and surrounding plantations—as the locals called the cotton fields—sporting their loads of boisterous teenagers, honking frequently. Drivers hollered out the windows at their friends, boasting of how they'd thump the other team.

As we strolled along the side of the road, Leon and I told the children about the football games we'd attended back in high school. I was kind of dating the boy who was the head cheerleader, and rarely missed a game. Leon's family had little money to spare, so he worked selling candy to earn his spending money. The first time we bumped into each other at a game, he said, "Aura, what are you doing here?"

Finding the question a bit silly, I said, "Watching the game, of course."

"But Jewish girls aren't interested in football."

"This one is," I answered, and we both laughed.

I loved going to those games when I was a teenager. I knew all the players and cheerleaders and half the band. It was a big party, and my friends and I danced in the stands whenever the band played the top hits of the day. Later, once Leon and I were sweethearts, we went to Harvard football games. All his friends were jealous that his girlfriend actually knew what was happening on the field.

We hadn't been to a game since college. Connie was quite the athlete, playing every sport available to girls, but of course she didn't play football; that was unheard of in those days. Philip was still in junior high and hadn't really shown an interest in sports. So I was looking forward to our first football game in Mississippi. Walking down the road, holding hands with Leon while we talked of our youth, my natural optimism took hold and I began to look forward to our future in Mound Bayou. Everyone around us seemed happy and boisterous, and the joy in the air was contagious.

Once we passed the elementary school, the hardtop ended and the road turned to dirt. Then I saw the football field, and it wasn't a stadium at all. It was downright shabby. While the grass was freshly trimmed, it was all brown, and the painted yard lines were fading and hard to see. Rusty metal bleachers stood on the spectators' side, while old wooden benches sat across the way, near the fifty-yard line, for the players. My heart sank a little, but I resolved to have a good time. The team didn't need a fancy stadium to play, and I didn't need one to watch.

Leon and I climbed up into the stands, along with the three children. Philip jiggled his knee up and down with nervous energy, and Charles, drawn by the salty smell of freshly popped corn, wanted to check out the food stand. Jo kept jumping up to see over the people in front of us, hoping to find some of her new friends and begging to be allowed to wander behind the stands, where other children were running about. I inhaled deeply as people around us started to open up their picnic dinners and the sweet scent of Southern barbecue wafted through the air.

My jaw dropped when the school band took the field to play the national anthem before the game. What a contrast with the dilapidated setting! Their bright blue uniforms were magnificent and looked freshly pressed. Every band member played in key, and they all marched in perfect synchronization.

The cheerleaders and crowd went crazy when the Mighty Hornets took the field. By halftime, our team was up seventeen to six and spirits were high. The marching band took the field and played "Goin' Out of My Head" as the High Steppers danced about, tossing their batons, and the drum major flourished his cape.

During the second half, the tension rose as the other team came on strong and scored a touchdown on the kickoff, narrowing our lead to only four points. We answered with a field goal, but with forty-nine seconds left on the clock, the opponent was threatening to score yet again to tie the game. Our defense held them to a field goal, and JFK won, twenty to sixteen. Everyone stood as the band played the school song and the crowd sang along: ". . . to the white and the blue, we'll always be true. JFK, we love you."

The lady standing next to me leaned over and said proudly, "That was written by our band director, Mr. Strickland."

"Very impressive," I answered, raising my voice so she could hear me above the crowd.

"You're Dr. Kruger's wife, right?"

"Yes," I said, watching Leon as he walked away from the stands, already engaged in conversation with several men.

"It's a good thing he's doin', comin' here to take care of folks."

"Thank you. I'm proud of him."

"We are too. Well, y'all have a good night. It's time to get those little children of yours home."

With that, she turned to the lady on her other side and started talking before I could ask her name. So instead I climbed down from the stands, gesturing to the children to follow. We caught up with Leon and began the brief walk home to our new trailers, during which I told him about that conversation.

"You should have seen her face, Leon," I said. "She really seemed happy that we're here."

"Why wouldn't she be?" he answered.

"Sometimes I worry about whether people really like us, whether they think of us as outsiders."

"Of course they think we're outsiders. We are. But that doesn't mean they don't want us and the clinic."

Jo (10 years old)

Today we went to our first football game in Mound Bayou. I'd been looking forward to it all week. I always wanted to go to the high school games back in Boston, but Mom and Dad never had time to take me. It's exciting living in a small town where we can do stuff like this. My folks are trying so hard to fit in that we would have gone even if we were still living at the motel in Cleveland.

All my new friends from St. Gabriel's were there, even the ones who live outside of town in the cotton fields—"out in the rural," as they say here. The guys I've started playing football with after school—Clarence, Toda-Jack, and Flit—had told me that they always toss the ball around behind the stands. Toda, whose real name is Alvin, had said he'd bring the football.

I got bored pretty soon after the kickoff. I like playing football, but it turns out that watching it is kind of dull. So I climbed down to look for my friends. I found some older boys —maybe fourteen or fifteen years old—throwing a ball around behind the stands, but I didn't know any of them. So I asked if they'd seen Toda or Flit or Clarence.

"Look at what we got here," the tallest one called out. "What's your name?"

"Jo."

"Y'all a boy or a girl?" said another one. I think they were confused because my hair was too long for a boy but I was dressed in hand-me-down clothes from my older brothers— jeans, a baggy T-shirt, and sneakers. Plus, they'd never heard of a girl named Jo.

"Feel that hair," the first one said, touching my hair and rubbing it between his fingers. I'm used to that by now, because it happens a lot. Folks here have never touched a white person's hair before, and they're curious. I let my friends at school do this, but this time was different and I got scared. I started to back up, thinking it was time to run, but I backed right into one of them.

"Hold on there, Whitey. Don't keep us guessing. Are y'all a boy or a girl?" Before I could answer, the first boy pushed me down. I hit my head on the ground, hard, but I was so scared that I barely felt it. "Let's find out. Pull his pants down." Then one of them held my arms down while another unsnapped my pants. I kept thinking, This can't be happening.

I tried to yell out to the other kids milling about behind the stands, but my voice wouldn't work. So I just kept kicking and managed to get free before the boys could do anything else. Then I ran away from them as fast as I could, snapping up my pants while I ran. I didn't even realize I was bawling until I heard one of them calling after me, "Let the crybaby run back to Momma and Daddy."

I stood next to the stands, pretending to watch the game, until I could breathe easily again. I kept looking around, thinking that everybody had seen and would be laughing at me, but nobody seemed to notice. I thought about telling Mom and Dad what happened, but that would only make it worse. Just thinking about talking to them about it is embarrassing.

Aura (45 years old)

The glow I felt as we left the football game stayed with me for the walk home. Leon and I held hands as if we were young lovers, and we chatted enthusiastically about the game and the town. Now that we were here, somehow Leon and I had again become partners and best friends.

As we walked in the front door, I heard the phone ringing. "Oh, Leon, they must have finally connected our phone." It was the perfect end to a wonderful evening.

I rushed to the kitchen to answer, hoping it was my parents. It was. The moment I said hello, my father bellowed harshly, "What kind of a town do you live in?"

"What are you talking about, Da—"

He cut me off, his anger clear even 1,500 miles away. "You must be out in the middle of nowhere! I've been trying to reach you for three days."

"I know, Dad. We've had our phone since we moved in, but—"

"Then why didn't you call?"

"That's what I'm trying to tell you. The phone was here, but it wasn't working. I'm sorry."

"I've called every day, and all that silly operator would tell me was that you weren't connected yet."

"That's right."

"Then tonight she said that your phone is working but there was no point in putting the call through, because you weren't home. Who does she think she is? When I call, I expect her to ring the house."

"I'm really sorry, Daddy, but we weren't home. We were at the football game."

"That's what she said, but I didn't believe her. You haven't been to a football game since you were in college."

"I know, but that's where we were. The whole town was there. That's what people do here on a Friday night. It was wonderful!"

"Well, I don't like it. She has no business screening your calls."

Poor Dad! Mound Bayou was a small town with a small-town telephone office and three-digit phone numbers. Not only could the operator listen in on phone conversations, she could also monitor the town's activities by looking out her second-floor window onto the main street. She hadn't just guessed that we had gone to the football game; she'd seen us walk by. Dad couldn't appreciate the humor of the situation, and his sour mood spoiled the evening for me. Leon tried to cheer me up, but I couldn't let him. All I wanted to do was retreat to our bedroom and read myself to sleep. I'd never quite outgrown being more affected by my father than I was by my husband. Since the early days of our marriage, I'd followed my father's lead, even when I knew that it bothered Leon. At my father's direction, I'd even hidden the fact that he worked for the Jewish Mafia from Leon. I justified my silence in the same way in which Dad justified his work to me, saying that he wasn't really doing anything wrong—all he did was run a lottery that he believed would one day be legal and managed by the state. Only later did I learn that when Leon found out, he felt suckered into marrying into a crime family and never quite forgave me for that deception.

FIVE

INSPIRED *to* TEACH

Cooking Class--- Mrs. N. W. Norman, Instructor

Speech and Drama --- Mrs. A. K. Kruger, Instructor

Let us think of education as the means of developing our greatest abilities, because in each of us there is a private hope and dream which, fulfilled, can be translated into benefit for everyone and greater strength of the nation.

—JOHN F. KENNEDY

September 1967
Aura (45 years old)

The children were less challenged academically than they would have been had we stayed in Newton. Within a week of our arrival, Sister Rosarita declared Philip too advanced for eighth grade and recommended that we move him to the public school and push him ahead a year. I worried that he'd feel lost there, but he adjusted rapidly and soon began developing friendships not only with his classmates but also with some of the older students.

Jo complained that she was bored, that the students were still learning their multiplication tables, something she'd mastered two years earlier. Leon's solution was to buy a set of self-paced math books that would teach her algebra. She loved studying math the same way that Leon did, and the two of them bonded over her studies, spending hours each week exploring concepts and working on problems.

Of the three children, Charles seemed to like school the most. Sister Rosarita took the time to talk with him about issues he found important—philosophy, literature, culture—and never dismissed his comments because of his youth, but instead took him seriously. She appreciated how widely read he was for an eleven-year-old and encouraged him to tackle ever-harder material. Charles still had difficulty following directions and staying focused, but the nuns were somehow able to reach him in a way his teachers in Newton hadn't been able to.

While it warmed my heart to see how he loved his

teachers, I ached when I got reports of what a loner he was at school. He rarely interacted with the other children, preferring to bury himself in a good book. But he raved about Sister Rosarita. One night, though, he said, "I think I made Sister Rosarita mad today."

I felt myself tensing up. "Why do you say that?" I asked.

"What did you do?" said Philip, implicitly assuming that Charles had done something wrong.

"I didn't *do* anything," Charles responded indignantly. "I only asked her how she could believe everything in the Bible."

"What makes you think that made her mad?"

"Because she wouldn't talk about it, and she'll talk about anything. She shut me down, just saying, 'I'm a nun.'"

"Well, she *is* a nun," said Jo, jumping into the discussion. "That's not shutting you down."

"Maybe not. But when I told her that wasn't a good enough reason, she got upset."

I sighed inside, just imagining how rude Charles would have seemed. I knew he wasn't trying to be disrespectful, but he had a way of challenging people that came across as nagging, and nobody liked that. I loved his intellectual curiosity, but it did seem to get him in trouble, especially with his teachers.

Charles's next comment pulled me from my quiet reverie about his difficulties. "Then Sister said, 'My entire life is devoted to my faith, and you don't have the right to try to force me to question it. Don't you think I've had questions and doubts of my own?'"

WHILE THE CHILDREN SETTLED into their school routine, Leon spent more and more time at the clinic. With the arrival of the building modules, he faced an unending list of tasks. Unconstrained by the tightness of their temporary quarters in an old church parsonage, the doctors were able to see more patients and better address their problems.

Leon was fascinated by the new work, so much more interesting to him than his old pediatric practice. Although the clinic planners had expected most of the patients to be children and had thus hired pediatricians, it turned out that the majority were elderly. Instead of childhood illnesses, Leon and his colleagues were treating arthritis, heart conditions, and malnutrition. Each morning before dawn, he sat at the dining room table with his old medical books, reading everything he could about diseases of the elderly. He loved being a student again, even without a teacher. He'd earned the nickname Happy Hacker while in college because he'd gotten such a kick out of doing his homework.

Most of his patients suffered to some extent from poor nutrition as a result of the dreadful poverty of Bolivar County. Despite that, they dressed up in their Sunday best to come to the clinic. A few days after it opened, I was sitting at home with my needlework when a knock at the front door broke the quiet. I was surprised by the sight of an elderly man in a black suit, the black dress hat he held in his hand giving him an air of Sunday service. He handed me a note written on a page from Leon's prescription pad. It said, *Please feed.* As he mumbled, "Doc said I should give you this message," I took another look at him and realized how painfully thin he was, his cheeks caved in and the loosely hanging suit completely thread-worn. He'd been to the clinic because he felt weak, and Leon had realized the man was hungry. Eventually, the clinic would have a food bank. But since that was still a couple of months away, Leon had sent him to me. The scribbled note was his attempt to maintain his patient's dignity. Instead of saying that he was sending the man to the doctor's wife for a meal, Leon had asked, "Would you mind bringing my wife a message?" and, knowing that the man couldn't read, hadn't even bothered to put his note in an envelope.

"Thank you so much," I said, instinctively maintaining the deception that he was helping us. "I was just about to have lunch. Please join me."

He hesitated, clearly drawn to the thought of a real meal but nervous about entering a white person's home.

"You'd be doing me a favor. I hate eating alone." Then I walked across the porch, pausing at the sliding glass door to glance back. He didn't move.

"Come on in. Lunch is waiting."

As I slid open the door, I was relieved to see him take a few steps toward me. "Don't be shy. The dining room is just through this door."

As he took a few hesitant steps toward me, I held out my hand to him. "Can I take your hat?"

Handing it to me without a word, he entered our dining room and stood staring at the painting over the sideboard. "My parents gave that to me. I remember it hanging in our dining room when I was a small child."

"Yes, ma'am," he said, finally breaking the silence he'd maintained since he'd first told me about the note. "It's a mighty fine picture."

"I'll be just a minute. You sit here and relax while I make us some bologna sandwiches."

While I worked in the kitchen, I could hear him tapping nervously on the table. I started to pour us each a glass of milk and then remembered that it might be hard to digest, and so instead got some water from the jug we kept in the refrigerator.

After sitting next to him, I asked, "Do you live in town?"

"No'm."

I waited for him to elaborate, but he remained silent, staring at his plate.

"Was today your first visit to the clinic?"

"Yes'm."

After that, I gave up on trying to get him to talk. I'm such a slow eater that he finished long before me, but he didn't stand up to leave; instead, he waited patiently, looking about the room, continuing to avoid eye contact. The moment I was done, however, he reached for his hat, which I had placed on the sideboard, and said, "Thank you, Miz Kruger. I sho' do 'preciate this meal." Then he backed out of the dining room, turning away only after he'd made it to the front porch.

That night over dinner, as Leon and I relayed our halves of the story of our day, I said, "It felt good to be helpful."

"What do you mean?"

"I like to be needed."

"Of course you do," he said. "It's not good for you to spend all your time just sitting around."

"I'm not," I protested, feeling as if he were blaming me for not making better use of my time. It seemed unfair, given that he was the one who had pulled me away from my job working for my father's restaurant, my duties in his office, and the volunteering I did at the children's schools. "I'm writing letters and reading and doing needlework."

"That's not enough. You need something more."

"What else is there?" I asked, frustrated by his seeming lack of empathy for my situation. "It's not every day that I can make lunch for one of your patients. And you won't let me work at the clinic."

"We've been over this. It's not that I don't want to. I can't."

"I know. You've hired nurses and clerks, and you need to give the jobs to the folks in the community." I waited for him to disagree with me, hoping he might suggest a way I could work with him. What he said instead left me speechless.

"Why don't you look into teaching?"

"What?" I stammered, stunned by his suggestion.

"They have a shortage of teachers at the high school. And you'd be great at it."

Though terrified at the idea of teaching, I could feel myself smiling at the compliment and couldn't help but fish for more. "Why do you say that?"

"You're patient with teenagers, and you love literature. You could make it exciting for them. Some of them can barely read. You could change that."

"The school would never hire me."

"Sure it would. I wasn't going to tell you this, but I've already spoken with the superintendent about it." Leon waited for me to agree, certain that it was the best thing for me. But I found the prospect too scary to say a word.

"Come on, Aura. You've always admired Jo from *Little Women* and said you wanted to be a teacher. Now's your chance."

"That was different. She was more of a mother to the students. It was her husband who was the teacher, Leon. I wouldn't know what to do."

"Sure you would. Just give it some thought."

At first I ignored Leon's suggestion, fearful that I was woefully unqualified. The longer I sat about with nothing to do, however, the more I contemplated making a change. Lost in thought, I tried to envision myself in front of a classroom. Every time I did so, a sense of panic welled up deep inside. Back and forth I'd go, sometimes thinking I could be a good teacher, more frequently worried I'd fail miserably.

Fortunately, the first step was taken out of my hands. Answering a knock at the front door, I was greeted by a man saying, "Hello, Mrs. Kruger. I'm Curtis Jones and I'm the superintendent of the Mound Bayou schools. Can we talk?"

Inviting him in, I asked, "What can I do for you, Mr. Jones?"

"I want you to teach over at the high school."

"What do you mean? Teach what?"

"Dr. Kruger tells me that you majored in English in college."

"That doesn't mean I can teach it, just that I know something about it."

"That puts you ahead of many of our teachers." Then he explained that much of the coursework that I'd had in high school was more advanced than what he'd had in college.

"Look, Mrs. Kruger, your husband warned me that you'd say no. He said that you'd be a great teacher but didn't know it yet. He also told me that the only way you'd come give it a try is if I came over and begged you. So that's what I'm doing. Please, Mrs. Kruger, we need you. We truly need you."

For every objection I raised, he had a reason why I should give it a try. Finally, worn down by his insistence that I would be a fine teacher, I asked him what time I should come the following morning.

"Why wait until tomorrow? Can't you come right now?"

"I . . . I'm not dressed for school."

"You can change."

Seeing that he was staying put until I agreed, I told him that I'd get ready as quickly as I could and would meet him at the high school in less than an hour. Even that wasn't fast enough. He said he was going to wait in his car, and then I could follow him to the school as soon as I was ready.

It wasn't until a few days later that Leon admitted that not only had he talked with the superintendent about it, but he'd also encouraged Mr. Jones to recruit me. "Don't wait for her to come to you," Leon had said. "Stop by the trailer and tell her that you need her. And don't take no for an answer."

❧

"WELCOME TO JFK HIGH SCHOOL," said Mr. Jones, leading me in from the parking lot. "Let me show you around a bit, and then we'll get you started."

Our first stop was the office, a small room just to the left of the main entrance. Although the lady working behind the counter was pleasant enough, the room was institutional, dreary. No posters brightened the concrete-block walls. Although everything was clearly brand-new and clean, the school didn't feel welcoming. The halls were eerily quiet with all the students sitting behind the closed doors of the classrooms. In the library, every seat was occupied. Some students slept with their heads on their arms, others stared at the ceiling, some chatted quietly. A few were reading or studying.

"This is why we need more teachers, Mrs. Kruger," Mr. Jones said.

I nodded, not getting his point.

"We have this beautiful new building but not enough teachers. So these students just sit here doing nothing."

"All day?" I asked, somewhat incredulously.

"Not the same students, of course. We rotate them through."

"That doesn't sound so bad. I can remember spending one period each day in the library. We studied or read."

"One period would be just fine. Most of these students are here longer than that. Now that you're here, some of them can go to class instead."

With that, he walked me to my new classroom. It was a modernly equipped foreign-language lab; each desk had its own set of headphones. But with nobody on staff who spoke another language, the room had apparently remained empty since the school had opened, a couple of years earlier. No scuff marks on the walls or floors, no bulletin boards with colorful posters of faraway lands. The blackboard looked as if chalk had never touched it. The only sign that anyone had used the room at all was a large brick holding the door open.

"Make yourself at home here, and I'll be back in five minutes with your students."

I stood at one of the windows, staring out over the parking lot. My hands found their way to my face, holding on as if to provide support. I had no books, no supplies, and, most frightening of all, no curriculum. Should I perform monologues from Shakespeare that I'd memorized back in college? Tell them stories from great American literature? Before I had a chance to decide, students began to file into the classroom, heads down, shuffling their feet, silent. Only one girl made eye contact with me, timidly looking up and smiling. At that moment, that small gesture of friendliness meant the world to me.

Each time I thought everyone was inside, more students would arrive, quietly walking. No jostling in line, no dash to get the seats in the back row or by the window, no shy smile from a boy hesitant to let the girl beside him know he liked her. Nothing.

Then it clicked. Something Leon had told me a few days earlier became painfully clear. Many of these students had never seen a white person up close. They'd been raised to fear white people, to always appear docile and unthreatening, to avoid eye contact. If they behaved in any other manner, they risked trouble.

As I looked out over the sea of faces, I panicked as I discovered that they all looked the same to me. *I know I'm not prejudiced*, I thought, trying to convince myself. *But how can I teach them if I can't tell them apart?* My heart pounded, and I had difficulty breathing. All the boys had crew cuts. The girls wore their hair straightened in updos, and their dresses and skirts were uniformly conservative, just above the knee. The boys mostly wore dark pants and collared shirts. A few were barefoot. Everyone had dark brown eyes and black hair. I searched for Afros, thinking those students would be easier to remember, but not a single one sported the style that had grown popular in the past couple of years as a statement of Black Power.

After a few frantic minutes, I realized that I would have to look for other ways to tell my students apart—the shape of a face, body build, height. I even noticed that although the students were all black, they had many different skin colors, ranging from a golden tan to a dark ebony. I hoped that maybe if I memorized their names, the rest would follow. I took a deep breath and introduced myself.

"Welcome to class. My name is Mrs. Kruger. I've just moved here from Massachusetts, and my husband is the medical director of the new clinic being built out on Township Road. My oldest son just transferred into the ninth grade here, and some of you may have met him. My two youngest children attend St. Gabriel's . . ." I trailed off. Did they think that I thought my children were too good to be in the public school? "Now I'd like each of you to tell me your name and a little bit about yourself."

I looked around for some paper to take notes on and discovered that the desk was completely empty. Fortunately, I was in the habit of carrying a pen and notepad in my purse. As I dug around for them, I turned to the young man sitting in the front row by the window, but he looked down at his desk, silent. I waited. He waited.

"Why don't we start with you telling me just your name?"

He glanced up at me for only a moment. Then he mumbled something I couldn't understand.

"Excuse me," I said. "I couldn't hear that. Could you say your name again?"

He repeated himself, a little bit more loudly.

"Was that 'Larry'?"

"No'm." He tried again, but I still couldn't get it. Finally, I walked over to his desk and asked him to spell it for me. I couldn't even understand him saying the letters of the alphabet. But after several painful efforts, I finally recognized the name Leroy and then moved on to the next student.

I gave up on getting them to tell me anything more about themselves. They spoke the same English I did, but their dialect was so pronounced that I could barely catch a word they said. As I worked my way around the classroom, one name after another was unfamiliar to me: Fragepani, Tyree, Annyce, Sanfeur. I quaked inside, wondering if I'd ever be able to teach them anything. It was only the first hour of the first day, and already I was floundering. It took me the whole period just to walk around the room and record their names so that I could make a seating chart.

As that class ended and everyone walked out into the hall, Mr. Jones arrived with a new group of thirty. "How did it go?" he asked.

"Can I be honest?" I responded.

"Of course. What's on your mind?"

"I can barely understand them. I've heard that many of our students dream about going north one day and finding work in Chicago, but how are they going to be able to do that when the people doing the hiring won't be able to understand a word they say?"

"I see," he said, squinting his eyes and drawing out the phrase as if he were nervous about where I was going with this line of thought.

I desperately wanted Mr. Jones to know that I respected him and the students, but it seemed like once again I'd said and done the wrong thing. I quickly decided that I couldn't afford to worry and plowed ahead with my idea. "I can help with that. I can teach them how to modify their speech patterns so that they can be understood anywhere in the country."

He finally smiled. "I think that sounds just fine, Mrs. Kruger. You let me know if there's anything you need to make that happen."

With that, he turned away, and I realized that my students were all sitting quietly, waiting for me to start class. This time I was able to get through all the names a little more quickly and had a little time at the end of the hour to introduce the phonetic alphabet.

"I assume you've all heard of the royal family in England," I started, happy to see a couple of students nodding. "They are the elite of the upper class."

When I saw the glazed look on many of their faces, I realized that the word "elite" might not be part of their vocabulary. I'd have to be more careful about my choice of words. Deciding to let it go this time, I walked to the blackboard and picked up a ruler I'd seen earlier lying in the tray underneath. I held it upright in front of me, saying, "If this ruler represents the classes of society, where is the royal family?"

"At the top," one student called out.

"What was that?" I asked, not quite understanding him.

He just looked down at his desk, not willing to risk another outburst, in case I was mad. "Please. I know you said something important. What was it?"

"They be at the top."

"Yes. And the poorest people are at the bottom. Is it any different in America?"

No response.

"Don't we have a society in which everybody is equal?" I rotated the ruler to a horizontal position. "Here in Mississippi, there are no classes. Everyone is protected equally under the law. We're all the same. Right?"

I waited. "Don't you agree?" I asked, hoping someone would be brave enough to say no. Finally, I saw a girl shaking her head.

"Doris," I said, glancing at my seating chart, "why are you shaking your head?"

Doris looked younger than some of the others, perhaps because of her heavy glasses. She wore her hair short and parted on the side, a less sophisticated look than the styled appearance of most of her classmates.

"We ain't all equal, ma'am," she whispered, barely loud enough for me to hear.

"I think you're right," I said, smiling to show my appreciation of her willingness to speak out. "So we're not a classless society."

Then I held the ruler vertically again, saying, "Without speaking out loud, imagine where you would place yourselves on the ladder of American society. Nod when you've picked a spot on the ruler."

Once they all indicated that they were ready, I said, "Now let's talk. Who do you think is at the bottom of the ladder?"

"We are," mumbled Roy, a thin boy with a high forehead and close-cropped hair.

"Are you sure about that?"

"Yes, ma'am," he said, with a little more force.

"What about the American Indian? Do you think he might be worse off than you?"

Nothing but blank stares.

"He lives on a reservation, right?"

A few nods.

"Where it's almost impossible to find a job."

"And the white folk, they took the land away from dem," called out Elizabeth, a girl with a great big smile and very dark skin. Her smile disappeared quickly when I looked at her, and she bit her lower lip as she realized what she had said, worrying that I would find it offensive.

"That's right," I said. "They were here first, and yet we forced them off their traditional hunting and farming territory. Does that seem right to you?"

"No," spoke up Roy again. "But they is still better off than us."

"You may be right. All I ask is that you keep an open mind. But whether you're at the bottom of the ladder or close to it, what can you do to move up?"

More silent stares. One boy looked up at the ceiling, while another gazed out the window. I knew I'd have to say something challenging if I wanted to capture their attention.

"You're already doing it. You're getting an education. And that's the best way. But we can do something even more specific than that." I paused, partly to see if they were with me and partly to think carefully about my wording so that I wouldn't inadvertently insult them. "We can learn to speak in a way that commands respect. If you learn to speak like the majority of the population, you'll have a better chance of landing good jobs.

"Now, I want you to imagine that we're learning a

brand-new language. You'll talk the way you always have when you're at home and with your friends, but you'll use your new language for school and work."

Having noticed that most of the black people I'd met over the last few weeks pronounced the word "ask" as "aks," I decided to start there. "Let's begin with the word 'ask,'" I said. Glancing at my seating chart again, I called on a girl who looked a little bit sleepy: "Naomi, I want you to repeat a word for me."

She pointed to herself, as if to say, *What, me?* and I nodded. "Please say the word 'ask.'"

"Aks."

I looked around the room. "Can anyone hear the difference between what I said and what Naomi said?"

My heart pounded in my chest as I wondered if I'd ever be able to get the students to respond.

"Fragepani," I said, choosing another name and wondering at its similarity to the pretty flower frangipani.

I heard giggling from a trio of girls sitting near the window.

"Did I say something funny?"

"No, ma'am," answered Fragepani, looking down at his desk. "But my name is Frag."

"Okay, Frag. Can you hear the difference?"

"No, ma'am."

"Listen again. 'Ask.' 'Aks,'" I said, writing the phonetic spelling on the blackboard.

"'Ask.' 'Aks.' Look at how they're spelled phonetics. And see how my mouth moves differently with the two words." They stared at me, but I didn't see any glimmer of interest, no heads nodding, no sign that they understood.

I sighed internally, frantically trying to figure out how to capture their imagination. "Let's try something different. I want everyone to hiss like a snake. Don't be shy. With me. *Sssss.*"

A few started to hiss.

"That's it. But I need everyone to join in. Let's make the students in the next classroom think we've just released a whole nest of snakes."

"*Sssss,*" they all hissed, laughing at themselves.

"Great. That's the sound in the middle of the word 'ask.' The next step is to put the sound 'a' before the hiss."

A boy in the back of the room experimented softly —"Asssss"—and then let out a loud guffaw.

As I walked toward their desks, they were suddenly quiet, their eyes growing large, fearful that I'd be mad at the disrespect. Instead, I said, "Congratulations, gentlemen. You've figured it out." I could feel the whole class relax.

Then I walked back to the front of the room and wrote "asssss" on the blackboard. "Now let's all say it together. Asssss."

Amid much laughter, the whole class repeated after me. As the bell rang to signify the end of class, I said hurriedly, "All you have to do now is put a 'k' at the end of it, and you have the word 'ask.'"

Then the bell rang again and it was time for lunch. The principal, Alvin Moore, showed up at my door. "Miz Kruger," he said, stepping into the classroom, "how was your morning?"

I found myself grinning from ear to ear. Although I was still nervous about whether I could be a good teacher, the morning had flown by and I'd had a lot of fun. I was an actress at heart, and here I'd had the chance to take center stage. And I wanted to let myself believe that I'd captured my audience, that they'd responded to me. At least they hadn't sat mutely staring down at their desks, as they had done initially. It was a start.

Before I could answer Mr. Moore, he said, "It's lunchtime. I'll show you to the cafeteria."

It was jammed with several hundred students, their voices creating a cacophony. Despite that, the room had air-conditioning and felt bright. I inhaled the delicious smell of beans cooking and realized how hungry I was.

All the teachers sat together at one table. After we went through the food line, Mr. Moore took me over and introduced me to everyone. There was Jackie Lewis, a woman who looked so young that it was hard to believe she wasn't one of the students. There was a couple who looked to be in their early thirties, the Windhams. He taught shop and she taught typing. I received the warmest welcome from Mary Gates, the school librarian, who said, "I'm always happy to meet an English teacher," as we shook hands. Then she added, "You'll meet my husband later. He's the principal of the junior high across the street."

The beans were delicious, but I avoided the fatty pieces of salt pork, even though they provided much of the flavor. I could barely tolerate the bitter collard greens that everyone else seemed to like so much, but I ate them, not wanting to remind anyone that I was a Northerner, an interloper. It was hard enough dealing with the stealthy stares as students and teachers alike glanced my way, curious about the only white person in their midst.

Over lunch, Mr. Moore told me that the last period of each day was devoted to enrichment, specifically the fine arts and athletics. Mostly, that meant football and band practice. But there was a theater class as well. Given that I'd minored in drama in college, he suggested that I help with that.

I looked forward to the theater class all afternoon, picturing the exciting rehearsals at which Leon and I had worked together in high school. I wondered what play the students were doing and whether they'd already memorized their lines. I was dismayed, however, when I arrived to find the students just hanging around and talking. The three teachers were doing the same. I sat in the back, watching, trying to figure out how I might help and feeling inadequate for the task. How could I as a beginning teacher tell these others how to run a drama class?

I brainstormed with Leon about it over dinner and thought about it while falling asleep that night. For the next few days, it was all I could think of when I wasn't teaching my English classes. Finally, during my conference period a few days later, it came to me.

I was sitting in the small teachers' lounge, where we could relax for one hour out of each day. It was a dark room with no windows, one couch, and two chairs. I was there at the same time as Mary Gates, the librarian who had been so nice to me that first day at lunch. She and I had begun a warm friendship, based on our shared optimism and a drive to do what was best for the students.

Mary wasn't much taller than I was and had light skin and a hint of gray showing in her hair. She looked serious most of the time, befitting the person responsible for keeping the students quiet in the library, but when she smiled, her eyes lit up. And she smiled whenever we talked about literature.

"What do the students read, Mary?" I asked. "I've been encouraging them to talk about books in our speech classes, but it's like pulling teeth."

"That may be because a lot of them won't read. They'll sit in the library for an hour and just stare out the window."

"Do they know how?"

"Oh, most of them can read some."

"Do you think they need a remedial reading class?"

At first, Mary looked at me without responding. After a moment, she nodded and said, "That would help. But I'm not sure that a lot of them would be willing to try."

"I'll figure out a way," I answered. "I'm going to talk to Mr. Moore about it and see if he'll let me do that instead of helping out in the drama class."

By the time I approached him with my idea, I'd given a lot of thought to Mary's concern about getting the students interested. "It wouldn't be like a regular English class," I explained to Mr. Moore. "Students would have to volunteer for it, and I don't want to have any grade other than pass/fail, so they're not intimidated."

Mr. Moore said yes before I finished speaking. Then I made one last request. "I'd like to use the choir practice room above the stage, where no one would know we were there. That way, the students won't be embarrassed."

"Whatever you say, Miz Kruger. I'll ask the teachers to announce it in homeroom tomorrow morning."

The next day, I walked across Township Road to the elementary school and picked up some third-grade readers, believing the students would need to start with something easy. The books were filled with simple stories about a wide range of topics. There was one about a pudgy bear in Yellowstone Park. Another described a donkey and a dog playing together on a farm. Each story introduced a handful of new vocabulary words, like "cub," "pudgy," and "jealous."

Armed with my new books, I waited at the end of the day in the choir room, not knowing what to expect. I stared at the blank gray walls and rearranged the furniture into a circle. I paced back and forth across the front of the room, stopping occasionally to listen for footsteps. Fifteen minutes went by, then twenty. I wanted so much to help, but what could I do if the students wouldn't even show up?

I was almost ready to give up when I heard some noise in the hall. A burly young man poked his head into the room, looked around, and then disappeared. A moment later, he stepped in, followed by eight more. "We on the football team, Miz Kruger. Coach say we need to come read wid you."

"He said he'd bench us if we don't," another player added.

"Take a seat, gentlemen," I said, relieved that I had some students to teach, even if they weren't there by choice. "Coach Lambert is a smart man. How many of you want to play football in college?"

Almost every hand went up.

"And do you think you'll graduate from college?"

"We don't care 'bout that, Miz Kruger. We just want to play ball."

"Well, you should care," I said, leaving no room for disagreement. "Have any of you read *Sports Illustrated* magazine?"

One of them laughed. "Naw, we just look at the pictures. We cain't read."

I smiled back. "That's why you're here. Well, there was an article just the other week about black athletes just like you getting scholarships to play sports in college."

"All right!" said one of the boys, not quite getting where I was going.

"It would be all right, except that what happens is that the players work hard for the team until they use up their eligibility or get injured. Then their scholarships are taken away and they're sent on their way without a degree. In many cases, they still can't read or write. When you get to college, you demand a real education. Don't let anybody just let you play football and never go to class."

Several of them shuffled their feet nervously, not sure how to respond. "You can't read well because the system has failed you, not because you're stupid. You *can* learn to read. You've just never been given the proper opportunity."

Then I handed out the books I'd picked up at the elementary school and asked for a volunteer to read. No response. If I'd asked for someone to go out for a long pass, nine hands would have shot up. No one would have been fearful about dropping the ball or looking bad in front of his teammates. But reading out loud was another story entirely. Their fear of failure had frozen them. Silently, I wished that somewhere in my education, someone had showed me how to teach remedial reading.

"Let's start with something you know. Am I right that all of you can write your own name?" My pulse slowed down a bit when I saw them all nodding. I could do this. "Great. I'm going to pass around a pen and paper for you all to write your names. That way, I'll know who you are.

"And the alphabet? Do you know the alphabet?" Again,

everybody nodded. My excitement grew as I started to believe this was going to work.

"Okay. Now, I want you to relax for the moment and just listen. I'll do the reading, and you can try and follow along. See if you recognize some of the letters and the sounds they make. It's okay to point to the words, if you find that helps." With that, I began reading the first story, looking up frequently to see if the students were following. A few were, but most were just watching me, more interested in hearing the story than in trying to read. It was like reading to my own children when they were barely more than toddlers.

The next day, hoping that easier material might make them more willing to try, I returned to the elementary school and found some second-grade readers about Dick and Jane playing with their dog, Spot. It worked. The football players were more daring. After I read a page out loud and pointed out how to recognize some of the oft-repeated key words, like "see," "run," and "play," Eddie was willing to give it a try. Sounding out the words slowly and carefully, he read, "See Spot run. Run, Spot."

"That's wonderful, Eddie," I exclaimed. "Who else is ready to read a line?"

⁂

IT WAS TWO WEEKS LATER, and the third-period bell sounded. As the students were settling in, I started to explain the day's lesson. Suddenly, the room was absolutely quiet except for my voice, and my students all turned to stare at the doorway. Two girls in the front row cringed and raised their arms to protect their faces. Everyone else froze.

When I turned to see what they were looking at, I saw a slender young man in a crumpled white shirt, the anger on his face warping what would otherwise have been a handsome countenance. He was brandishing the brick that moments earlier had been holding my door. He looked ready to throw it at any instant. I was furious. Who did he think he was to threaten my students that way?

Before I could react, he shouted, "I'm gonna git you," pointing at one of the students in the second row. "Ain't nobody be messin' wid my family."

My heart was pounding, but I was in charge and my students were counting on me. I walked right up to him and said, "Put that down! That's my doorstop!" My head barely reached to his chest. His face was all adrenaline and perspiration while he glowered down at me and raised the brick a little higher, as if getting ready to strike. For a moment, I felt as if I might have supplanted my student as his potential target, but I stood my ground. "Put it down now," I said firmly. Then I held my breath as I waited to see what he would do.

The boy looked down at me, our eyes locked together as we both stood frozen. Gradually, the fierce expression on his face faded to one of astonishment. "Now," I repeated, my voice still sharp. Then he slowly lowered his arm and put the brick back by the door. As I felt my students begin to calm down, I placed my hand on his arm, and said, "What's your name?"

"Rivers," he answered, gritting his teeth.

"And what's the problem, Rivers?" I asked, still touching him lightly to try to calm him down.

Pointing at one of my students, Rivers said, "He be messin' wid my brother."

"I understand how that would make you angry," I said. "But you can't just throw bricks at people." No response. "Can you?"

He shook his head slowly, still not looking me in the eye. "Rivers, would you be willing to come back after school so we can talk about it? Maybe we can figure out a better solution."

This would have worked with one of my own teenagers, but how was this potentially dangerous young man going to respond? My heart pounded as I realized how easy it would be for him to pick up the brick again and strike me. But I kept smiling and waited.

Finally, he nodded and walked back out into the hall. My students breathed a collective sigh of relief. They were all scared of Rivers and had never seen him back down so easily. I held my finger to my lips, indicating that they should stop chattering about what had happened, and we got on with the class.

By lunchtime, the whole school knew about it. Even the teachers were talking about it. One of them put down his fork and said, "You're wasting your time trying to talk to him, Mrs. Kruger."

Another jumped in, saying, "He'll never show up after school. You'll see."

Then the first added, "But in case he does, you better not be alone. There's no telling what he might try to do."

"He won't attack me," I answered. "If he'd wanted to do that, he could have hit me with the brick."

It was hard, later that afternoon, to not keep hearing their voices as I waited, wondering if Rivers would appear. And if he did show up, would I be in danger? I didn't let myself think about the possibility. Earlier that day, when I had walked over to Rivers without hesitation, thinking only of protecting my students, it had been life-altering. The threat had been significant, yet I'd handled it. Somehow, having faced down the terror of the moment, I was purged of fear for myself. I hadn't had time to feel afraid, and I'd gotten through it.

And so while I waited, whenever thoughts of danger started creeping into my imagination, I braced myself, focusing on how much I wanted to help Rivers. He was, after all, just a boy, not much older than my sons. Maybe, just maybe, with the right attitude, I could reach him. If only he would come talk with me.

And he did.

I invited him to sit down. I could feel his eyes following me as I took the chair next to him. He looked surprised, clearly not having anticipated that I would sit so close, rather than staying behind my desk, its bulk serving as a barrier between us. I didn't want that barrier. I wanted to demonstrate that I trusted him and, more important, that I cared. "Talk to me, Rivers," I said.

No response.

"What happened earlier today? What made you so angry?"

"Nothing."

"I don't believe that. You said that someone was messing with your brother. But throwing a brick? Surely you know that was wrong."

"I got a terrible temper, Miz Kruger," he said, looking down at his hands as if he might find an answer there. Remembering the Jim Crow custom requiring blacks to look down in the presence of whites, I tried to break through his wall by taking his hand in both of mine. He tried to pull away, glancing up briefly with a look of surprise, but I held on tightly.

"Rivers," I said, "I know how easy it is to get mad, especially when someone goes after your little brother."

"I got to take care of him."

"It's good that you want to protect him. But you can't go around hitting people and throwing bricks at them."

"No, ma'am."

"Would your mother want you doing that? Is that how she'd want you to watch out for your brother?"

"I dunno."

"Would you like to hear my ideas?" He nodded apprehensively. "How about if you breathe deeply and force yourself to wait before reacting?"

"I can't do that."

"Sure you can."

"You mean like countin' to ten?"

"That's right. And while you're waiting, you can think about the kind of person you want to be and how you want others to think of you. Can you try that for me?"

"Yes'm. Can I go now?"

"You can go," I answered quietly. "But, Rivers, I want you to know that you can always come sit in my classroom to cool off. Even if there's a class going on, you just slip in the back and take a seat. You stay as long as you need."

SIX

>-

IF NOT US, WHO?

If not us, who? If not now, when?

—JEWISH FOLKLORE/ROBERT KENNEDY

October 1967
Aura (45 years old)

I frequently brought in newspapers and magazines in an attempt to teach my students about the world beyond Mound Bayou. A picture of James Brown, with the quote "Say it loud. I'm Black and I'm proud" stared down at them from one bulletin board. Robert Kennedy was pinned to another, below which I'd written the quote "If not us, who? If not now, when?" On a third board, I posted a picture of a black man in his early thirties, along with the question "Who is this man?"

For weeks, my students begged me to tell them, but I wouldn't, challenging them instead to look for him in the news and find out for themselves. One day, Cornell Holmes came in, saying, "I figured it out, Mrs. Kruger! I know who he is!"

"Yes?"

"It's Eldridge Cleaver."

I was delighted that it was Cornell who had figured it out. He was a dream student—a member of the honor society, a talented basketball player, and a hardworking staffer for the yearbook. I don't think I ever saw him without a smile on his face, despite the fact that his fellow students teased him for his earnest manner when it came to academics.

"And who is Eldridge Cleaver?" I asked, hoping that Cornell had done more than just identify the picture.

"He helped start the Black Panthers."

"That's exactly right." With that, I pulled out several newspaper and magazine articles I'd been saving for this moment and asked Cornell to post them up on the board by Cleaver's picture.

My students grew accustomed to my attempts to bring politics into our classroom and thus weren't surprised in early October when I began talking about the upcoming election. Bolivar County was divided into five districts, called "beats," for the purpose of overseeing public works. Mound Bayou was in Beat Three, along with a tiny black town called Winstonville and the city of Shelby, with a population of about five thousand, just a few miles north of us. In the past, the white citizens of Shelby had always determined who the beat supervisor was. It was an important position, for it controlled where and when garbage would be picked up and which streets would be repaired—public services that were supposed to be available to everyone in the beat but tended to be much better in the white communities.

At first I was disturbed, because my students seemed uninterested.

"Why should we care about that," asked one of the football players, "when nothing's ever gonna change?"

"That's right, Miz Kruger," added Cedric. "What difference can we make anyways? We're too young to vote."

He was a bright young man, the youngest of eight children. He'd learned at home that he had to speak up if he wanted to be noticed amid all those siblings, and as a result had a reputation for being somewhat outspoken at school. That surprised me, for in my class he was quiet, perhaps hesitant to engage with a white teacher. It had taken a few weeks of encouragement, but eventually he had become willing to question me. Now he didn't think twice about making eye contact and expressing his ideas.

"Don't you care about the civil rights movement?" I asked. Cedric nodded. "Civil rights workers have given their lives in an attempt to ensure that black people can vote without fear of retribution."

"We know dat, Miz Kruger, but dat don' matter none. We still too young."

"You may not be old enough to vote yet, but you can encourage your parents and aunts and uncles to vote."

"I dunno—"

"If every adult in the district votes, we can be heard."

"You really think we can get a black man elected to beat supervisor, Miz Kruger? You be dreamin'."

"You may be right. But if we don't start dreaming, we won't be able to make changes. Someday we'll have a black beat supervisor. And it won't just be in Mound Bayou where we have a black mayor."

I turned to Bernard Wilson and smiled. He was one of my sharpest students and grasped the significance of what I was saying. The son of college graduates and a devoted reader long before he found his way to my class, Bernard was a highly memorable young man. He could have been a player—as the students said—if that had been what he'd wanted, for the girls flirted incessantly with him. He cared about his appearance, dressing better than the other students, with his pants creased and his button-up shirt looking fresh. Although he clearly enjoyed the ladies' attention, he seemed more interested in hanging out with his best friend, Truman White, his polar opposite in many ways. Truman was the everyman of the class. He was of average height and not particularly handsome, yet he, like Bernard, attracted the interest of the girls. He spent so much effort pursuing them that his nickname was Chase.

When Bernard chose to speak up in class, everyone listened, for he often had a different perspective than the other students. He didn't do it often; he had a shy streak. For some reason, however, this day he was willing to speak out and express annoyance with his classmates for complaining that since blacks were in the minority, they could never win an election.

He said, "A lot of the time, we're actually a majority, but we just don't vote. Besides," he added, "even if we don't win, we have to make a statement." I knew then and there that I'd have to keep my eye on him. He was going places.

"Bernard's right," I said, looking for an example to illustrate his point. "Suppose the question comes up of repainting the town hall. More than half the people want to paint it pink, but a number prefer green. The pinks win the election, but since so many people vote for green, the town leaders decide to find a compromise and propose that a third color be selected instead."

After much discussion, the other students began to agree with Bernard and assured me that they'd go back to their families and make mothers and fathers and aunts and uncles all promise to vote. I thought it was so important that I repeated the lesson in all my other classes.

As the November election grew closer, I learned that much of the community was already registered, thanks to the efforts of previous civil rights workers, but many were still hesitant to vote. Tales of people being arrested and beaten for trying to vote still circulated widely—stories made more vivid by photos in national magazines showing police dogs attacking nonviolent demonstrators at sit-ins protesting such harassment. Despite that, I found it hard to believe when friends in Mound Bayou said that members of the Ku Klux Klan and the White Citizens' Council were still willing to kill to prevent blacks from voting.

It suddenly became more believable and very personal when one night over dinner Leon told me how he'd provided medical care that day for a young teacher, a black woman who had been taken to jail and beaten for the crime of encouraging her students to stand up for their rights— a crime that I committed myself every day in my classroom. Only then did we really understand the need for volunteers to escort voters from the surrounding communities to the voting booths at our high school. One man drove while another held a rifle out the window, and the voters rode in the backseat. Mr. Wilkes, the carpenter who had built our porch a few weeks earlier, boasted that he was such a good shot, he could drive with his own gun out the window and could thus carry an extra passenger.

The morning bell hadn't rung yet on Election Day when I glanced out my classroom window and saw a car pull up. The passenger in front was the first to get out, holding his shotgun ready. After looking around, he leaned back into the car, presumably telling the others that all was clear. Then he escorted them into the building to vote.

A few students had started to come in for class, and I called them over to the window so they too could observe. As we stood there, another car pulled up and more voters walked into the building, again protected by a volunteer with a shotgun. Rivers Washington came up beside me and pointed out that there were several other men scattered about the parking lot, keeping watch.

"Miz Kruger," he said, "next time I'm gonna be out there too, makin' sure dat nobody gets hurt. We gonna make sure everybody votes. That's what we gonna do."

"What do you think you would do, Rivers, if somebody tried to stop you? Would you shoot?"

"Wouldn't need to. Nobody gonna mess wid me if I got a shotgun."

I hoped he was right. I cringed to think what would happen if one of the black escorts shot a KKK member who got in the way of the voting. Fortunately, the day passed peacefully, and the next morning, the news was out that the black man running for district, or "beat," supervisor had been elected. No longer would the area's black neighborhoods receive inadequate services like trash pickup.

My students were ecstatic, exploding with excitement at this turn of events. Some even thanked me for telling them to encourage their parents and aunts and uncles to vote. Their appreciation made me finally feel a part of the Mound Bayou community. Other things did as well. People began to invite us to various gatherings, to church, even into private homes. The postmaster and his wife, Preston and Pauline Holmes, became our bridge companions. Highly respected throughout the whole region, their family had been in Mound Bayou for generations. Preston's grandfather had started up the town's first cotton gin, and the two of them were leaders in their church. Their willingness to open their home to us and to dine in our home did much to help others accept our presence in town.

The more we were accepted, the busier we grew. Weekends, especially, were a treat. Blacks came to Mound

Bayou from miles around to enjoy the freedom of spending a night on the town without fear of being harassed by the KKK. One Saturday night, the local Elks club hosted a dance. Remembering our countless evenings dancing together in homes, school gyms, the Totem Pole Ballroom in Newton, and elegant hotels, Leon and I couldn't wait. Nothing was going to keep us away from the party.

The Elks Lodge was only a few blocks from our trailers. Despite that, we took the car because I was wearing my favorite high-heeled dancing shoes. As we pulled into the dirt parking area, we saw dozens of lights strung outside the old wooden building, creating a festive glow. Inside, all the guests were dressed in their Sunday best, the women wearing hats worthy of an Easter parade and the men wearing black suits with freshly ironed white shirts and skinny black ties. The hall was decorated with flowers and streamers. We hardly noticed that the tables and chairs were falling apart, that the un-air-conditioned room was hot and muggy, the floor sticky with spilled beer. We didn't care. We were going to dance.

We looked around for friends but saw nobody familiar. Maybe the townspeople would come later, but this early in the evening, it seemed as if everyone there was from out of town. It didn't matter. I could already feel my feet twitching to the beat of the live big-band music. It may have been the 1960s, but in Mound Bayou in the Elks Lodge, it was still the music of the 1940s, the music we'd danced to all through high school, the music of our youth. My heart soared.

Without even waiting for our first round of drinks, Leon jumped up and grabbed me and pulled me onto the dance floor, where we stayed the entire evening. We held each other close for the slow numbers, but when the rhythm picked up, Leon spun me every which way and others stopped dancing to take in our fancy footwork.

About half an hour after we started, Leon noticed some newly arrived friends watching and said, "What do you say, Aura? Let's liven things up."

With that, he pulled me back to the table and asked another woman to dance. For a moment I was annoyed, fearful that I'd spend the next three hours watching Leon dance with everyone but me. But just for a moment. Almost immediately, a stranger asked me formally, "Would you do me the honor?"

Without a word, I stood and took his hand. Before long, he was twirling me under his arm and the time flew by. Then Leon danced up to us and we switched back. Within seconds, another stranger tapped Leon on the shoulder, saying, "May I cut in?" and didn't wait for a response. He grabbed my hand and whirled me about. I looked around and saw Leon dancing with another woman I didn't know.

After folks saw that we were having a good time and ignoring the fact that we were the only white couple there, we found ourselves in high demand. The women were eager to have Leon ask them for a dance, and the men lined up to be my partner. At one point, a man cut in, seeing only a woman who was a good dancer and having fun, and he was a little too drunk to notice at first that I wasn't black. All of a sudden, he did a double take and glanced rapidly about the room, a frightened look in his eyes. I smiled warmly to reassure him, and he finally smiled back. "Ain't I in Mound Bayou?" he asked. "They ain't no white ladies in Mound Bayou. Is you white?"

A bit flustered by his question, I could only nod, to which he shrugged his shoulders and said, "Can't be. You must be black."

November 1967
Jo (10 years old)

We've been living in Mississippi for a couple of months now, and we're getting used to it. It hasn't really been all that hard. I play with the kids in the neighborhood, just like I did in Newton, but I had to stop playing football. It seemed like every time I got tackled, some boy was trying to put his hand up my shirt. Not Clarence or Toda-Jack or Flit, but some of the others, who I don't know as well. Now I shoot baskets instead.

But it bugs me. I don't like it that I can't do what I want. That never happened in Newton. Maybe it was because I hadn't grown yet, but I don't really believe that. It's just different here. I can be walking down the street, minding my own business, and some teenage boy will reach out to grab me, even if Charles is with me. It's like they think it's a game. They don't do it, though, if Philip's around. I guess he's big enough that they don't want to get in trouble for messing with me.

Other than that, I'm mostly having just as much fun here as I did before we moved. School's not as interesting, because I already know a lot of it, but Dad started teaching me algebra, which is pretty cool. I wouldn't have started that for a few years back at my old school, so I guess I'm actually getting ahead. Dad tries to work with Charles too, but they just end up mad at each other.

I like working math problems more than when we read

plays out loud. That's what we're doing so that Philip doesn't get too far behind. We started with *A Raisin in the Sun*, because it was the first Broadway play to be directed by a black man and written by a black woman. And then we did *The Merchant of Venice*. I couldn't really understand either one, but Philip seems to like it and even asks when we're going to read next so he can find out what happens, so I don't want to complain.

Philip spends more time with me here than he did before—I guess because he doesn't have as much other stuff to do. He's been teaching me how to play the recorder, and sometimes we play duets sitting on his bed. I think we sound pretty good. And Auntie Helen sent us some sheet music for the piano, oboe, and flute, so we've been practicing that too—with Charles on the piano, Philip on the oboe, and me on the flute. Our neighbor Mr. Garmond said he thought he was listening to a record when he heard us playing and couldn't believe it when he looked in the window and saw that it was just us. It's a little strange to think of him looking in the window. Nobody did that back in Newton.

Charles is kind of afraid of him because sometimes he gets drunk and pounds on the side of the trailer in the middle of the night, hollering out stuff like, "Hey, Doc! What you doin' in there?" I don't hear him too often, because his house is next to the other trailer and he stays over on that side most of the time. Mom tells us to just ignore him, that he's harmless, but Charles isn't convinced. One time, Mr. Garmond actually leaned a ladder against the trailer and climbed up on the roof and started running around up there. I thought it was funny, but Charles found it terrifying. I think he just gets scared more easily than I do.

I did get frightened the other day, though, when I'd gone with my friend Glen and his mom to the grocery store in Cleveland. She said we could play on the toy horses in front of the store. We didn't have any money to make the horses move, but we were still having fun. Then some lady grabbed me by my arm and pulled me off the horse and said, "Does your mother know you're playing with a black boy?" That's not actually what she said. She used the N-word. But I can't bring myself to repeat that. Even back in Boston, we were taught how disrespectful that word is.

Anyway, when I said, "Yes, ma'am," she asked where I lived and started to nod when I told her. Then she said, "I've heard about your family. You better clear out of here before my husband comes by and makes you stop messing around with that heathen. Now get out of here."

After that, we ran into the store and stayed close to Glen's mom. I kept looking around for that lady's husband, but he never came by.

It's kind of funny. Mom talks a lot about our being accepted into the community here in Mound Bayou, but the people in Cleveland sure don't seem to like us much. And when it comes down to it, I'm not sure all the kids in Mound Bayou do either. Sometimes they tease me about being Jewish and call me Christ-Killer. I've stopped raising my hand at school because it seems to make my classmates mad when I know so many of the answers. Mom and Dad say I should just sit quietly so that other kids can have a chance. I don't mind—we all have to help out— but sometimes I wish I didn't have to worry so much about saying the wrong thing.

SEVEN

꧁

IF NOT NOW, WHEN?

Black is beautiful.

—PHRASE POPULARIZED IN THE CIVIL RIGHTS MOVEMENT

November 1967
Aura (45 years old)

We were frequently invited to church on Sunday—despite being Jewish—and tried to rotate through the different churches so as not to offend anyone. Usually I'd go on my own, since Leon often worked on Sunday mornings and the services were too long to interest our children. The local children, however, all attended with their families, their Sundays completely taken up with the religious traditions of the community. The children always seemed to grow restless but were quickly quieted by one of several women who stood guard in the aisles, each with one hand resting on the back of her waist while the other waited, poised to intervene the moment a child's attention wandered too far.

I never found it difficult to pay attention, for every preacher in town was a dynamic speaker and the services were punctuated with old-time hymns sung in a gospel-blues style. I was sometimes asked to speak during the service about the importance of education. On one Sunday, the minister introduced me by saying, "I want y'all to listen closely to Miz Kruger, because she speaks from the heart. There is so much love in her house that even the cat never leaves the yard."

That day, I spoke about the hippie movement and the ever-widening gap between teenagers and adults. I challenged the parents to recognize that it had grown tougher to be an adolescent than when we were young. The clear guidelines and expectations we faced made it easier to know what to do. Today's youth, on the other hand, had so many choices to make that it could be overwhelming. Most of the faces of the congregation looked tired from their harsh lives. Despite having been handed a difficult situation, however, they generated a remarkable energy, and their willingness to listen to what I had to say somehow reenergized me. I had been asked to speak to inspire them, yet they were the ones inspiring me. I closed with something I thought was critical: "It is our job as parents and teachers not to criticize our youth for their independent thoughts, but to encourage them on their path toward adulthood. I'm impressed with your children as I watch them in my classroom. I enjoy working with them. And I love them. Thank you for having enough faith in me to trust me with them."

After church, I stayed for the potluck social, just as I always did when I attended a service. These dinners were a mainstay of Mound Bayou's social life. Folding tables were set out in the meeting room if the weather was bad, or outside on sunny days. The women all brought their favorite dish, having hoarded food all week so they'd be able to show off their cooking talents. There was sweet-potato pie, the best fried chicken I'd ever had, and vegetables cooked in salt pork. And it wasn't just the women who cooked. One man boasted that nobody could make fried fish taste as good as he did, and then invited us all to a fish fry at his place the next weekend.

Unfortunately, food was not that plentiful for my students the rest of the week. One day when we were waiting for the last bell in school, I overheard a girl say to a friend, "I can't hardly wait to git home—we're gonna have meat for the first time in months!"

When her friend asked, "What kind of meat?" she said, "Salt pork in the collards," and I pictured the tiny piece of pork fat I always removed and threw away from a can of beans.

In addition to lacking adequate food, many of my students owned only one set of clothes, and all too often that didn't include shoes. In good weather, they would come to school barefoot. In winter, they'd cover their feet with rags held on by rubber bands. One young man was embarrassed to come to school because the only pair of pants he owned was too small for him. We had a long talk, and I reminded him that who he was and what he made of himself were far more important than what he wore. When he seemed unconvinced, I told him that he should be proud. After all, it was easy for most of the other students to come to school, but because he often missed school to work in the cotton fields, he had to work harder to stay caught up with his studies. I wouldn't let him leave until I got him to hold his head up high, look me in the eye, and tell me that he was proud of himself.

November 1967
Jo (10 years old)

Last night was Halloween. We'd brought our costumes with us from Newton because Mom had said we might not be able to find new ones in Mound Bayou. She was right. We could've bought them in Cleveland, but none of my friends did that. When I tried to make plans with them to go trick-or-treating, they looked at me like I was crazy. "That's for babies," they said. "Besides, nobody's got a costume anyways."

That was enough for me. I didn't want to go if my friends weren't going. But Charles talked me into it. He's so persistent that he can pretty much talk me into anything. He was dressed like a hobo, and I had a Frankenstein mask and costume. We took some flashlights and some brown paper grocery bags for the candy. At first we stuck to the paved part of Township Road and it was just like in Boston. But once we left the main street, it was really quiet. Nobody else was going door-to-door.

It was kind of eerie. I wanted to just go home, but Charles said we ought to try and get more candy, so we knocked on a door and waited. Nobody answered, but we could hear voices inside. I was about to give up when a lady opened the door. As we said, "Trick or treat," I looked past her and saw a single bare light bulb hanging from the ceiling. Looking confused, she said, "I'm sorry. I don't have any candy for you."

I couldn't quite figure out what was going on, but Charles understood immediately. He said, "That's okay. Take ours in case any more kids come by." Then he handed her his bag and told me to do the same.

We didn't talk about it on our way home. I felt badly that we seemed to have embarrassed the lady. We should never have gone trick-or-treating. I wish Mom and Dad had stopped us from going out, but I guess they didn't know either.

February 1968
Aura (45 years old)

Soon after Christmas, the weather turned cold. One morning I woke up to discover several inches of snow on the ground. Instead of appreciating the beauty of it, I was overwhelmed with a sense of sadness at the thought of my students trudging through the snow with rags on their feet. How were they going to manage? They would be shivering in their unheated shacks with the wind blowing through cracks in the walls. At least once they arrived at school they'd be protected from the weather.

Charles and Jo didn't notice that I was upset. Snow! They grabbed their winter coats and ran outside to play, to build a snowman and have a snowball fight before breakfast. They roamed the neighborhood, looking for friends, but the streets were deserted. Eventually the children gave up and returned home to eat.

In between mouthfuls of cereal, Jo asked, "Why weren't the other kids outside? Are they afraid of the snow?"

As I explained how their friends didn't have the warm jackets they did, their excitement melted away. They were learning much about caring for those less fortunate. Philip, at fourteen, was learning the fastest. He'd always been highly political, enjoying debates with his grandfather over current events. Leon and I were thus not surprised when he began to join his friends in an attempt to integrate some restaurants in Shelby.

The first time they tried, a man stopped them at the door, saying they weren't welcome there. He backed off, however, when the teenagers said that since the bus depot serviced interstate traffic, it legally had to be open to everybody, including black people. But when Philip and his friends sat down to order food and coffee, they were quoted prices ten times higher than usual. Realizing they didn't have enough money to pay, they decided to try a different restaurant, where they had greater success.

Many of the adults in town found the teenagers' activities distressing and feared retaliation from the white communities in nearby towns. Most were even upset when I encouraged students to think of themselves as black instead of Negro. Shaken out of my naiveté, I learned a lot about politics that year. For example, one local bigwig had been given land near town to plant food for his family in exchange for keeping others quiescent. People feared that if they rocked the boat, they'd lose their jobs and their families would starve. Even though blacks owned and ran the town, the white power structure still had tremendous influence.

Philip began to get a reputation as a troublemaker. One time, when he and his friends were walking in Shelby, a white police officer stopped them and told Philip to get in the police car. We'd been warned when we first moved to Mississippi that many of the police were KKK members and that under no circumstances should we let ourselves be picked up. Philip, remembering that advice, refused. His friends moved in closer, creating a barrier between him and the officer. By the time the policeman worked his way through the group, one of the boys had extricated Philip and was already driving him back to Mound Bayou.

When Philip told us the story over dinner, I didn't know what to say. How could I reprimand him for putting himself at risk, when I did that every day in the classroom? But he was only fourteen! And he wasn't in the classroom, safe in Mound Bayou, where everyone knew us and for the most part accepted us. He was in the next town over. I wanted to tell him to stop, that he was too young. But I couldn't. And it wasn't just because in a way I was proud of him and pleased that he was following in my footsteps. It was also that, deep down, I knew I couldn't stop him if I tried.

AT SCHOOL, I CONSTANTLY sought to expose my students to music, books, and plays written by black people, wanting to instill in them the "Black Pride" that was sweeping the nation. The phrase "Black is beautiful" was heard frequently in my classroom, and my students were thus surprised one day when they walked into my classroom and saw on the chalkboard in bold letters the statement "Black is not beautiful." The objections started before the bell rang.

"Miz Kruger! How can you write that? All year you've been telling us that black *is* beautiful."

"Is it?" I asked, as they looked about, confused.

"The color black has come to symbolize unpleasant aspects of life in many cultures throughout the world. In the early days of humankind, cavemen were afraid of the night, fearful of the cold and dark that came with the setting sun. Later, we see this fear reflected in religious writings."

"You mean like in the Bible?"

"That's a great example. Where do we see this in the Bible?"

"God cast a plague of darkness on the Egyptians when they wouldn't free the Jews."

"That's right. And tell me something: What color do you think of when you think of heaven?"

"White."

"And hell?"

"Black."

"Do you still think black is beautiful? In almost every society around the world, the color black evokes feelings of melancholy and despair, of alienation and evil. White, on the other hand, is usually viewed as symbolic of virtue and purity, of truth and spirituality."

"That may be true, Miz Kruger, but all that stuff has nothing to do with us, with who we are. We are beautiful."

"Yes, you are indeed beautiful," I answered, my eyes tearing up. I had reached them. They were beginning to believe that their beauty was tied not to the color of their skin but to who they were inside.

For the next few days, they wrote about being black. After reading their essays, I felt a need to do something more. Over dinner one evening, I had a brainstorm. "Leon, let's take my students on a field trip to Memphis to see the movie *Guess Who's Coming to Dinner.*" Released just prior to the holidays, it had been banned in Mississippi because it presented interracial marriage in a positive light. Not only would the students have a wonderful time, we could also discuss the content of the movie, along with the political ramifications of having to go all the way to Memphis to see it.

Leon and I helped chaperone two busloads of students, many of whom had never been much beyond the city limits of Mound Bayou. The two other teachers had been to college in Jackson, so it wasn't a new experience for them, yet they seemed to be enjoying the adventure as much as the students. The ride north was filled with the chatter of excited young voices.

As we approached downtown Memphis, however, all the passengers grew quiet as they stared at the tall buildings. Although only seven or eight stories high, they were significantly taller than the two-story structures the students had seen previously. "Miz Kruger," one girl asked, "how do people get up dem high buildings? Does they have to walk up all dem stairs?"

"Sometimes they do," I answered, "but only when the power goes out. Usually they ride in elevators."

"What's an elevator?" asked one student.

"I seen them on TV," answered another. "It's a little room that goes all the way up to the top."

"That's right. And sometimes, if you're going up only one or two flights, they'll have something called an escalator. That's like a staircase that moves and carries you up."

"Can we ride on one of those, Miz Kruger?"

Several others chimed in, begging us to stop at one of the "skyscrapers," but I told them we wouldn't have time, that we were expected at the theater any minute. "Is the theater going to be just like the one in Cleveland, or will it be in one of dem high buildings?"

"It'll be bigger than the one you're used to, but with an important difference."

"What's that?"

"You can sit anywhere you like."

"Don't they have a colored balcony?"

"They do, but I told them we wouldn't come if we had to use that. So they're putting on a special showing of the movie, just for us. We can walk in the front door and sit on the lower level."

The bus buzzed with astonishment. This was unheard of. Movie theaters throughout the South were still segregated. Either they didn't allow blacks at all or they had a separate black balcony, one that typically was cleaned less often and sometimes even cost more than the orchestra seats.

"How'd you talk them into letting us do that?" asked

Bernard, quick to realize that something must have happened to create this opportunity.

"It's all about the money. They didn't want to turn down the opportunity to sell a hundred tickets in the middle of the week, so they met our demands."

"That's tellin 'em, Miz Kruger," called out Cedric. "We be jes like the Black Panthers!"

"It shows you the power of money. But listen to me, now. Just because you *can* sit all the way in the front doesn't mean that you should. Try to sit about halfway back, because that's where the view is best."

Just then, the buses pulled up in front of the theater. I couldn't have been prouder as I watched my students walk quietly in pairs—just as I'd asked them to do—their heads held high as they crossed a whites-only threshold for the first time in their lives. Although they didn't say anything about it, I believe the other teachers were just as proud. What a fitting introduction to a movie about a black man marrying a white woman!

We talked about the movie for days afterward, and I could hear them in the halls, singing the song that had played during the opening and closing credits, "Glory of Love.

Seeing an opportunity, I found my old sheet music and moved class to the choir room, where I played the song for my students on the piano while they sang along. We talked about the lyrics and what they meant, how we can face anything the world might throw at us if we have someone we love helping us.

I noticed that their dialect seemed less pronounced in singing than in speaking. More than that, though, the work we'd done with phonetics had made a difference.

Between that and the fact that I'd grown accustomed to their speech patterns, I no longer had any difficulty understanding them.

It was a short jump from song lyrics to poetry, an effective means of tackling literature in small doses. They enjoyed learning about rhythms and rhymes and thrilled at their early attempts to create poems of their own.

On Valentine's Day, I started the class by saying, "I have something special for you today." Then I read aloud Elizabeth Barrett Browning's sonnet: "How do I love thee? Let me count the ways. / I love thee to the depth and breadth and height my soul can reach . . ."

EIGHT

❧

WE SHALL OVERCOME

Racism is still with us. But it is up
to us to prepare our children for what
they have to meet, and, hopefully, we
shall overcome.

—ROSA PARKS,
WHO REFUSED TO GIVE UP HER SEAT ON THE BUS,
SPEAKING TO A REPORTER IN 1998

April 4, 1968
Aura (45 years old)

The front door slammed and Philip dashed in, shouting, "Mom! Mom!" The panic in his voice made my heart race. "Martin Luther King's been shot," he said, his voice breaking.

"Wh—? No," I said, staring at him in disbelief.

"It's true. I heard about it down at Mr. Crowe's barbecue."

My voice stuck in my throat, and I couldn't say a word. All I could do was shake my head as I felt my eyes begin to water.

"I was playing pinball when this lady came up behind me and said, 'You shouldn't be playing games, son. Dr. King's been shot. He's dead. Y'all go on home.'"

My tears turned to cries, and I kept saying, "No, no" over and over again. I could barely breathe, and then my words turned to wails. I had to get myself under control, for the children if nothing else. As I walked over to the phone to call Leon, I heard someone knock at the front door. My legs were shaking as I looked out the window to see who was there. A stranger—a tall, imposing black man dressed in a dark suit—stood with his hand poised, ready to knock again. "Philip," I said, my voice quivering, "could you see who he is?"

Drying my eyes, I took several deep breaths and then went to find out what our visitor wanted. He had remained outside when Philip had opened the door, but when he saw me, he reached forward to shake my hand and said, "Good evening, Mrs. Kruger. I'm a friend of your husband's, and he asked me to come over. Would you mind if I come in? I'd really enjoy a cup of coffee."

"Please," I said in a trance, still hardly able to talk. He followed me into the dining room, where I gestured for him to sit. "Make yourself at home. I'll be back in a minute."

I went to the kitchen to pour coffee for the two of us. As I returned with a cup in each hand, I saw that he hadn't settled at the dining table. Instead, he had placed a chair by the front door, positioning himself so that anyone looking in from the street would see him. He was there to protect us.

Close to midnight, Leon arrived home. I expected our sentinel to depart, but he didn't. Instead, he told us to go to sleep and he continued his vigil by the door. The emotional upheaval left us drained, and we slept soundly. When we awoke in the morning, the room was empty, our guest departed.

Our phone began ringing before daybreak. Calls came from all over, urging us to stay home that day. Friends and relatives spoke of the backlash of blacks against whites occurring throughout the country. Riots had broken out in over a hundred cities as word spread. Black mobs were burning white-owned stores and throwing rocks through windows, demanding to be heard. Those who cared about us were concerned that even the people we considered our friends might rapidly turn into enemies.

The first call came from Leon's boss in Boston. On the one hand, he wanted everyone to report to work so the clinic could operate smoothly. On the other, he worried that the white staff could be in significant danger. The next call, from my father, involved no torn loyalties.

Without a second thought, he demanded that we get in the car and return to Boston. When I told him we couldn't do that, he backed down and instead insisted we take whatever measures were necessary to protect his grand-children. As more people called, I wondered if the operator was listening in and whether she'd tell everyone in town what we said. Fellow physicians, friends, family all called with the same message: we should remain invisible for a few days, until common sense could be restored.

Over breakfast, Leon and I discussed our options. "I can't believe that anyone will harm us," I said.

"I agree," Leon said. "We'll be safe as long as we remain in Mound Bayou, where we know everyone and everyone knows us."

Yet fear lingered in the back of my mind. "What if we're wrong? What if someone attacks?"

"They won't," said Leon, "and I don't want to hide."

Neither did I. We had to go to work if we were to continue living in Mound Bayou. With that settled, we told the children that they'd have to stay home without us.

"That's not fair," protested Philip. "If it makes sense for you to go to work, then I should be allowed to go to school."

When both Leon and I refused, Philip persisted: "Don't worry. I'll be okay." Eventually, we gave in to his pleading and, having done that, decided that Charles and Jo could go as well.

A few minutes later, however, I questioned the wisdom of that decision as I stood outside the front door and watched the two younger children walking toward St. Gabriel's. Would they be greeted with hostile looks and threats of violence? I didn't really believe that was an issue, but my stomach felt queasy at the thought. I was less worried about Philip as he headed in the opposite direction, toward the railroad tracks, for I knew I'd be joining him at the high school in just a few minutes.

At school, the sadness in the air was palpable. Students roamed the hallways, quietly hugging one another, too distraught to prepare for class. As I moved down the hall toward my classroom, students kept stopping to embrace me. We couldn't talk—we'd get too choked up—so we just held each other tightly. Some students wept openly on my shoulder. I wept too.

Several students followed me into my classroom, where I found many more students than were scheduled for my first period. They all quieted down as I stepped to the front of the classroom and turned to face them. I tried to speak but couldn't make a sound. I looked down and held up one finger to tell them to give me a moment to regain my composure. I tried a second time, yet still no words came. All I could do was shake my head.

"Miz Kruger," said Johnny, one of the students who wasn't supposed to be there, "Mr. Moore, he said we could put on a memorial service. And we gonna do that. Can we use your room to get ready?"

Others called out in agreement. Truman added, "We want to use all those magazines you've been showing us, the ones with articles about the civil rights movement. We'll be needing them."

Finally finding my voice, I said, "I'd be honored if you'd use my classroom as your headquarters. You just tell me what you want me to do."

"We don't need your help, Miz Kruger. We gonna do all the work. You jes help us get word out that everyone should go to the gymnatorium at one o'clock."

The room buzzed quietly throughout the morning as the students designed an extraordinarily moving program, typed it up, and sent it to the school's print shop to make copies. I was so caught up in watching their preparations that my earlier fears receded to the background and I stopped worrying about my family's safety. It thus surprised me when Bernard said, "Don't be upset if you don't see Philip for a while."

"Why? What's he doing?"

"We sent him home to get his guitar and to put on a jacket and tie, since he's going to be with us onstage."

How kind he was to have anticipated my fear and headed it off before I'd even had a chance to notice Philip's absence. I thought about all the calls we'd received earlier that morning. Those people would never understand what was going on, how safe we were, why we had no choice but to face the day with our friends.

A little before one, I walked into the gym and took a seat close to the front. The students, anticipating a large crowd, had set up every folding chair in the school. Within minutes, every seat was taken, yet people continued to pour into the room until they were standing shoulder to shoulder in the back. Those who couldn't fit inside the gym stood in the hallway, hushed so that all could hear. Some students had gone home at lunchtime to change into their church clothes. Parents and others from the community were in their Sunday best. Despite the large crowd, it was so quiet that I could hear the clock ticking. As I looked about, I realized that mine was the only white face in the entire crowd and would be until Philip appeared.

The service began with a song adopted as the Negro

National Anthem: "Lift Every Voice and Sing." We all joined in as one of my students led the singing, her voice strong and true—an amazing feat of composure in this difficult time. A few moments later, the band played "Born Free." How ironic! In the late 1960s in Mound Bayou, Mississippi, freedom was in many ways still an elusive dream.

I cried when one of my students walked to the microphone to recite a poem that she dedicated to Dr. King. She began speaking slowly, letting her words ring out to the captivated audience: "How do I love thee? Let me count the ways." I knew she had first heard the sonnet just six weeks earlier. I was deeply touched to feel my love returned. I knew then that my efforts were making a lasting impression on my students, that they would remember and use what they'd learned in my classroom. And, perhaps even better than that, they were making a lasting impression on me.

Two hours into the memorial service, twenty students walked onstage, Philip among them, carrying his guitar. He stood to the side and accompanied the singers in a heartfelt rendition of "We Shall Overcome." As the last note died away, Philip slowly approached center stage and spoke into the microphone. "We'd like to sing this song again, this time with everyone joining in. Please rise and hold hands."

Two Days Later
Jo (10 years old)

After helping Dad dry the dinner dishes, I went to my bedroom to read. I was sitting at my desk when something hit the screen in the open window right next to me. It was a huge rock, the size of a grapefruit, and it stopped just inches from my head. My heart was pounding as I looked out the window to see what was going on. Then I heard a loud noise on our roof, almost like thunder. This wasn't our neighbor tapping on the side of the trailer, or even running across the top like he sometimes did when he was really drunk. I jumped back from the window, terrified. Then I ran to the dining room, hollering, "Mom! What's going on?"

Charles ran in from the other trailer, and then Mom yelled, "Get down" and started pushing us under the dining room table. Dad crept over to the window to see if he could see anyone, and then the phone rang. Mom crawled toward the kitchen to answer it. Dad screamed for her to get back under the table, but she ignored him, saying, "It could be Philip. He could be out there."

Charles and I cowered on the floor, hugging our knees, curling up as tightly as we could. I cringed every time more rocks hit. They were so loud against the metal trailer that we could barely hear Mom's end of the conversation.

"Are they my students?" we heard her ask. We figured out that she was talking to someone about the attack. How could her students do this to us?

The noise stopped for a moment, and then Mom came back to the dining room, half standing. "Get down, Aura!" Dad shouted. "They're still there."

As if to prove his point, the racket started up again, this time punctuated by the sound of a gun. For the first time, Dad hit the floor. At first I was afraid that he'd been shot and I screamed, but he was just getting away from the window. He rolled toward us and tried to wrap himself around all of us at the same time.

"That's not them firing at us," Mom said. "It's Earl Lucas." He was our next-door neighbor. "That was him on the phone.

He said there are a bunch of teenagers out in the field behind us, and he said we should stay away from the windows. He's going to try to scare them away."

"Is he going to kill them?" asked Charles.

"No. He's just firing over their heads to make them stop."

At that moment, we heard the sound of a different gun.

"Oh no," Mom cried out. "They're shooting back."

Then all the noise stopped. No more rocks. No more gunfire. The phone rang, and we all just stared toward the kitchen. Then Mom jumped up and ran to answer it. Dad tried to stop her but she pulled away. It was Mr. Lucas, calling to say the troublemakers had fled.

When Mom came back in to tell us it was over, Dad said, "What did Earl say? Is he okay?"

"He's fine. That second gun was his. He said he used two guns so they'd think there were two of them up there."

"It worked," Dad answered. "They ran away."

"I told Earl that he'd risked his life for us and asked what we could possibly do to thank him. Do you know what he said?"

"What?"

"He said, 'Aura, you risk your lives for us every day that you're here.'"

Aura (45 years old)

The week following Dr. King's assassination was bedlam not only for us but also for people across the nation, as the riots showed no sign of abating. Some of my students had televisions and watched the story on the news. Others heard about it in the bars on Saturday night and in church on Sunday. It was the major topic of conversation in all my classes.

"Miz Kruger," said one student, "it's unfair. We should be out there protesting too, but they ain't no white people in town for us to protest against."

"'Ceptin' the Krugers," laughed another.

"Y'all know what I mean. I need to do something, anything."

"They doin' something in Shelby," offered another.

"Yeah. I heard the students wanted to do an assembly like we did last week, but the principal won't let them. He say it too dangerous. He be scared the KKK will come break it up."

"That's right. So 'bout fifty of them picked up the school bus and turned it right around. Then they moved it onto the grass."

"I dunno 'bout that, but my friend told me that since they can't do an assembly program, they gonna march on city hall."

"When they doin' that?"

"Day after tomorrow."

"Maybe we could all march too."

⚓

WHEN I TOLD LEON and the children over dinner about my students' wanting to march, Philip said, "I already know about it. We're gonna make it happen."

"What do you mean?" I asked.

"We were planning it all afternoon."

"Philip, I'm not sure I want you joining this march. It won't be safe."

"Sure it will, Mom. The preachers are involved with the organizing, and they're making sure that everything's going to be peaceful."

"I don't know."

"You should come too, Mom. Some of the other teachers are marching."

ON THE DAY OF the march, the sky was a brilliant blue, the sun beating down on us as we waited in the JFK High School parking lot for everyone to gather before heading out to Shelby. Philip went off with his friends, and I rode with my fellow teachers. When we arrived on the outskirts of town, we parked the car and joined five or six hundred other participants, mostly teenagers. The organizers were walking about, telling everyone what to expect and explaining the route we would follow, starting in the black section of town, continuing on through the white neighborhoods, and concluding at city hall and the town square.

"Listen up, everyone," one man called out in a booming voice. We could have heard him even if he wasn't using a bullhorn. "Y'all has to get outta the street so we don't get in da way of no cars."

"Ain't no cars comin' over here," called out one teenager.

"It's the police cars he be worried about," answered another.

"Dat's right," said the man with the bullhorn. "The police be watchin' us, jes waitin' for us to do somethin' wrong so's they can arrest us, or worse. We ain't gonna let that happen, now, are we?"

The students quieted down, nodding in agreement. "We is gonna keep this a peaceful demonstration, jes like Martin Luther King would want."

As if on cue, nine police cars pulled up, their sirens off but their lights flashing, and took up the whole block. The few stragglers still in the street jumped to the relative safety at the side of the road. There were no sidewalks. The black part of town, where we had gathered, consisted of only five unpaved blocks. On one side were vacant, muddy lots, open to the cotton fields in the distance. On the other, small wooden shacks lined the street, each with a rickety front porch, furnished with one or two old rocking chairs. We stayed on the side with the shacks.

Trying to ignore the police cars, our leader picked up his bullhorn again. "I want y'all to pair up and walk side by side. These officers," he said, gesturing to the cars lined up right next to him, "they want us to be in a line, not walkin' in a big group."

I had read about this in a magazine article. By forcing the protestors to stay spread out, the police could see everybody and, what's more, have a clear shot at them. I swallowed hard as I noticed that in each car, an officer held a rifle pointed out the window. The dark, reflective sunglasses the men wore made it impossible to see where they were looking, and I felt as if they were all staring directly at me. In several of the cars, police dogs sat in the backseat, watching everything, looking fierce and ready to attack. Shelby must have pulled in officers and dogs from the whole region to come up with such a show of force.

Not wanting to give the police any excuse for violence, we did as we were told, lining up neatly in pairs and staying off the street. I could see Philip near the front of the line, standing boldly with his friends. He was easy to spot, as he and I were the only two white people marching. As I looked around to find someone I knew with whom to march, a tall young man, perhaps eighteen years old, came up to me.

"Miz Kruger," he said, "can I walk with you?"

"Do I know you?" I asked.

"No, ma'am," he said, somewhat formally. "My name is John, and I'm a senior at Shelby High." Then he added, "I've heard about you, and it would be an honor to walk with you."

As I smiled and nodded yes, he positioned himself between the police cars and me, using his body as a shield. In so doing, he put himself in significant danger from the police or anyone else who might be offended by us. His request to walk by my side had really been an offer to protect me.

The next order was shouted out. "Everybody hold hands with the person next to you, so's we can be sure to stay in line."

John inhaled sharply. In Mississippi in 1968, a black man could be killed for taking the hand of a white woman. He didn't know what to do. Without hesitation, I took the initiative and took his hand, showing the people all around us—and especially the police—that it was my choice to do so. I didn't want anyone thinking I was an unwilling participant. Toward the front of the line, Philip stood calmly, hand in hand with a young black woman.

The signal came, and we began to walk slowly down the sidewalk, the sun already high in the sky and beating down on us. I looked into the street and noticed that a police car stayed right beside my partner and me, the officer in the passenger seat pointing his rifle at my partner the entire time.

As we started to walk down the sidewalk, people on the porches began singing hymns; a singing elderly person occupied every rocking chair we marched by. They waved to us, cheered us on with their voices raised in song. Many cried.

I became so accustomed to the presence of our well-wishers that it struck me as odd whenever I saw an empty porch. I suspected that whoever lived there must have been out at work or sick, because otherwise they would have been watching.

What a change a few minutes later when we marched into the white section of town! It was a different world. Instead of dirt roads, there were paved streets lined with well-kept sidewalks. Rather than tiny wooden shacks, handsome brick and stone homes with manicured lawns stood alongside the streets. Instead of the warmth of voices raised in song, there was absolute quiet, with not a soul in sight, for the residents had locked up their homes as tightly as possible. Drapes were drawn shut, streets were deserted, the silence relentless. Every now and then, someone peeked through a curtain or openly glared.

We marched for close to two hours, crisscrossing the town until we'd walked down every block. Finally, we stopped in front of city hall and one of the ministers stepped to the front of the line. In a deep, booming voice, he said, "Let us all now bow our heads in prayer."

We stood as if in a trance, swaying silently back and forth. After a minute of silence, the minister spoke again. "We offer thanks, oh Lord, that the good people of Shelby have allowed us to walk peaceably through this town. And we pray that the leaders of this community, the men working in this very building, will open their hearts and stop the oppression of their black neighbors. We ask this in Jesus' name."

With one voice, the marchers responded, "Amen."

Resuming our march, we returned to the black section of town, where we stood in front of one of the churches, a small wooden structure with peeling paint. The students wandered off, but the adults gathered on the church steps, talking over the events of the day. Suddenly, over the chattering, I heard a deep baritone quietly singing "We Shall Overcome." One by one, the rest of us joined in. As if choreographed, we formed four lines on the church steps, standing close together with arms linked.

The police took notice. They pulled their cars up in a line facing us and turned off their motors. Sitting in their cars and staring, they pointed their rifles at us, just waiting for an opportunity to fire. We acted as if they weren't there and continued to sing for another ten minutes, verse after verse, gently defying them.

When we were all sung out, we walked right past that row of rifles and joined the teenagers, who had assembled in the town square. A number of people made speeches, after which Philip borrowed a hat and a dollar bill and stepped into the center of the circle. He held up the dollar and said, "There is Black Power. There is White Power. But also, there is Green Power. We are passing the hat. Please contribute whatever you can." The students then used that money to buy food to feed the crowd that gathered in Mound Bayou to celebrate at the end of the day.

When Philip and I arrived home, Leon greeted us with the news that my presence had so upset one of the onlookers that she had called Mississippi senator John

Stennis's office in Washington to complain about "those no-good Northerners marching right along with the colored folk."

"What?" I asked.

"He called me and actually threatened me with closing down the clinic. He said, 'You know the rules. You're not allowed to mess around with local politics. I'm going to shut you down and make sure you lose your funding.'"

"But you didn't march, Leon. Nobody from the clinic was there."

"I tried to tell him that, but he wouldn't listen. He said, 'I know you're involved. I just got a call from an irate woman who said she saw two white people from the clinic marching past her house.'"

"So what did you tell him, Dad?" asked Philip

"I said, 'I'm so glad you reached me directly, Senator Stennis, because I know what is really happening. There are indeed two white people marching—my wife and my son, neither of whom is employed by the clinic.' Then he mumbled something and hung up on me."

NINE

~

GUESS WHO'S GOING *to* COLLEGE?

Education is our passport to the future,
for tomorrow belongs to those who
prepare for it today.

—MALCOLM X, 1964, IN HIS SPEECH AT THE FOUNDING
RALLY OF THE ORGANIZATION OF AFRO-AMERICAN UNITY

Spring 1968
Aura (45 years old)

It was an unusually warm Saturday night in early May. Leon had been out all day, working an extra shift at the clinic, so I was pleased when he showed up after dinner, wanting to talk. I started for the living room, expecting that we'd sit there for an hour before bed, but he said, "Let's go for a walk. We haven't done that in ages."

I loved the idea. We used to stroll for hours when we were teenagers, solving all the problems of the world in our imaginations. Actually, Leon had done the solving while I'd listened. Now we really were making a difference, he at the clinic and I at school.

He took my hand as we walked out the door, and I leaned my head on his shoulder, enjoying the close camaraderie of the moment. As we approached the tracks, we saw the last few cars of a freight train speeding through town and were glad that we hadn't come out earlier; the trains were so long in Mississippi that you could wait forever for them to pass.

It was a busy evening in Mound Bayou. The lights were still on at Crowe's Bar-B-Q Kitchen, and all the tables were full. Several boys were standing around the pinball machine, taking turns testing their skill. The sound of their laughter escaped through the open windows, muffled only slightly by the music playing on a radio somewhere inside.

Traffic was heavy on Highway 61, with pickup trucks driving by, their beds filled with teenagers in search of a good time. Even the Laundromat was active, the ancient machines whirling through their cycles as women chatted nearby, folding their laundry.

As we passed the open doors of a bar, the sound of jazz playing on the jukebox caught our attention. Thinking we might dance, we ignored the smell of stale beer and made our way inside. Glancing about, I was upset to see two of my best students sitting at the bar, each with a drink in his hand.

Shaken, I turned to Leon and said, "They shouldn't be in here."

"Aura," said Leon, pulling me back as I tried to walk toward them, "they're almost men. You don't need to say anything."

"Yes, I do. What if it were Philip? Wouldn't you want someone to stop him from drinking?" Before Leon had a chance to respond, I slipped my hand away from his and walked over to speak with the boys.

They were talking quietly, their speech slightly slurred. "Good evening, gentlemen," I began. "I can't believe what I'm seeing."

"What do ya mean, Miz Kruger?" asked Truman, the young man whose fellow students knew him as Chase.

"We're just having a good time, ma'am. There's nothing wrong with that," Bernard added as he took another swig of beer.

"Yes, there is. You're much too young to be drinking. You're both far too intelligent to be wasting yourselves like this."

"Where else would we go?" asked Truman. "What else is there to do?" Then he smiled as if he'd just scored a point in a debate.

I tried to think of a rational response but was left

speechless. What could I suggest? Going to a movie in Cleveland at the segregated theater, where they'd have to sit in the "colored" balcony? Even if I'd been able to come up with some suitable entertainment for a Saturday night, there was still the larger issue—there just wasn't that much to do in Mound Bayou. Sure, they could become teachers, or work at the clinic or in the town's small retail community, but with the exception of those few jobs, there was no work except picking cotton or working at the cotton gin. That's why so many of my students dreamed of moving north to Chicago.

Leon and I talked it over as we resumed our walk. "I want more for my students than what they can get here. Bernard's a genius. He was reading Shakespeare long before taking my class. And Truman, he may not be as well read, but he has an intense desire to learn."

Later that night as I lay in bed, trying to fall asleep, the boys' words echoed in my mind: *What else is there to do?* Feeling powerless to do any more on my own, I tried to think of whom I could call for help. A wave of relief flooded me as I thought of my friend Leonard Zion. As the dean of undergraduate students at Brandeis University, he might be able to use his influence to create some opportunities for my best students.

I'd gotten to know Leonard two summers before, when Leon and I had enrolled in a two-week class at Brandeis. He'd participated in a panel on current events and impressed me with his comments. Toward the end of the evening, the moderator asked the audience for questions, and I stood up to ask about something that had been bothering me ever since I'd first read about it in the local paper.

"There was recently a high school prom in a suburb just north of Boston where all the students are white except for one black boy. When he asked a white girl to dance, the principal stepped in and sent everybody home. What would each of you have done if you'd been in charge?" I hoped that at least one of the participants would be brave enough to speak out against such behavior. I'd found it unnerving to learn of this discrimination right in my hometown. I was naive enough to believe that this sort of behavior was limited to the South.

Some of the panelists agreed with the principal. Others said nothing. Leonard, however, had the courage to say, "I think the principal was wrong. I would have let nature take its course."

After the panel discussion ended and we were all standing about, talking, he came over to me and said, "You were brave to ask that question."

I responded, "You were brave to give the answer you did. Aren't you worried about losing your job?"

He laughed, saying, "Brandeis is a special place. I'd worry about losing my job if I didn't speak out against discrimination."

That was the beginning of a close friendship. It was his creativity and willingness to stand up to societal norms that made me think he'd know what to do to help Bernard and Truman, so I called him first thing in the morning. After we caught up on each other's lives, I told him of my sleepless night filled with frustration over the plight of my students. "We need to find a way to break the cycle. Leonard," I pleaded, "isn't there anything you can do? Please think of something."

As I'd expected, he promised to give it some thought.

A few days later, he got back to me with exciting news. Not only had he come up with a brilliant solution to my problem, he had also taken steps to implement it. He had asked the university to accept three of my students on a full scholarship—including room and board—and Brandeis had agreed.

"What do I need to do? Do you need letters of recommendation? Applications? Just tell me and I'll make it happen."

"Aura, you don't need to do a thing. If you say these students belong at Brandeis, we're willing to trust your judgment. You just get them here in June and we'll take care of the rest. Just make sure they have warm clothes for the winter. I tried to get a clothing allowance for them, but it didn't fly. We'll tutor them over the summer under the auspices of our Upward Bound program and try to get them ready for their freshman year. And if they need a year of preparation, we'll even do that. All they have to do is sign a letter of intent."

Leonard had come through for me, for my students. Now it was my turn. I already knew I wanted Bernard and Chase to go. But Leonard had come through with three slots, not just two. Who should the third student be?

Cornell Holmes was an obvious choice. I hadn't worried about him the way I had about the other two, because I had a feeling that his parents would make sure that he went to college whether I helped or not. But once I'd found scholarships, I had to ask him. I was frustrated when he turned me down. "Mrs. Kruger," he said, "I can't leave my family like that. Everything I know and love is right here in Mound Bayou."

"I understand that, Cornell, but this is an amazing

opportunity for you. Don't you want to even consider the possibility? Perhaps talk it over with your parents?"

"No, ma'am. I've made up my mind."

Later, when Leon and I were playing bridge with Cornell's parents, Preston came as close to getting mad as I'd ever seen. "Tell me, Aura," he said, "why you didn't include Cornell in the group you're sending to Brandeis. Isn't he one of your best students?"

"Didn't he tell you?" I answered. "I asked him the same day the scholarship offers were made. He said he didn't want to go."

"How could you leave something this important to a seventeen-year-old to decide? You should have come to me."

My stomach tightened as I realized the mistake I'd made. Of course Preston was right. He and Pauline were my best friends in town, and their oldest son one of my most talented students. I'd had the opportunity to send him to college in New England and had botched it; now it was too late. Another excellent student, Joe Leggett, had already taken the third slot.

Truman had been the most hesitant of the three, worried about whether he could handle it. "Won't the classes be hard, Miz Kruger?" he asked.

"You'll certainly have to work, but they won't give you anything you can't manage."

"What about the other kids? What will they think about us black folk just showing up? You really think they'll be okay with that?"

It dawned on me that Truman couldn't imagine a college that both black and white students attended. "I know they will. Besides, you won't be the only ones."

"For real, Miz Kruger?"

"To be honest with you, Truman, I don't know for sure what it'll be like. Brandeis is a liberal place, but you may have some trouble fitting in. Some of your classmates might be scared or even hostile."

"But you think I can manage?"

"I know you can."

I knew I sounded more confident than I felt. They would not have an easy time. The academic challenge would be difficult, and the emotional challenge even more so. Uprooted from everything they'd ever known, they'd be thrown into an environment unlike anything they'd experienced previously.

I spoke at length with each of them, describing what they could expect when they got to Brandeis, both the good and the bad. All that remained was for us to obtain the money to buy plane tickets and suitable clothing. Unbeknownst to us, word of the scholarships had spread like wildfire, and before we had a chance to do any fundraising ourselves, the town's churches took the lead. It was a major topic in all the sermons the following weekend, after which a hat was passed and everyone in town donated something. These three young men represented the town's hope for the future, the possibility that the next generation would find opportunities where none had existed before. It wasn't long before they had enough money for clothes and plane fare and we could begin planning for their departure.

❧

AS THE SCHOOL YEAR drew to a close, my thoughts turned to my son Philip, fourteen years old and finishing his freshman year of high school. I still cringed at the thought of my students out drinking on a Saturday night and worried that it wouldn't be long before Philip began doing the same. Little did I know that he'd already begun.

I had other concerns as well. The education he was getting at the high school was in some ways equivalent to what he'd already received by the seventh grade in Newton. Philip was bright and already considering a career in law, and I wanted him to be able to hold his own at any of the top schools in the country. How could that possibly happen with the education he'd receive at JFK High School?

Complicating matters further, Philip didn't hide his interest in girls. He loved going to the school dances and wasn't timid about dancing. He smiled and flirted, and the girls responded in kind. I never saw this as a problem until Truman pulled me aside one day and said, "Miz Kruger, you got to talk to Philip about this. Some of the boys are getting mad at him."

"I don't understand, Truman," I answered. "What's he doing wrong?"

"Nothing. But prejudice works both ways. Some of the guys don't like it that a white boy is foolin' around with black girls."

I smiled at the thought of my fourteen-year-old son starting to date.

"This is serious, Miz Kruger," Truman said, more vehemently than I would have expected. "Philip could get in trouble."

"He's still a child and is just having fun. Surely the boys can see that."

"I don't think so. He's white and an outsider, and they don't want him doin' like that."

I felt as if I'd been punched in the stomach. We were still *outsiders*, unwelcome. I knew that Truman was trying to be helpful, but what he said was painful. More than that, it made me realize that we had to send Philip away.

Much as my heart ached at the idea of my boy leaving home, it ached even more at the thought of what might happen to him if he stayed. Leon and I began the painful task of looking for a new home for Philip, a home that couldn't include me. I was devastated.

It took about a week to really accept that Philip had to leave Mound Bayou before we were able to calmly consider the possibilities. Boarding school wasn't an option. Even if we'd had the money—which we didn't—our exposure to the poverty in Mississippi left us ill at ease with any expenditure we viewed as extravagant. As I was sharing my concerns with my daughter Connie during our weekly phone call, she offered to have Philip move in with her. Much as I wanted to say yes, I thought about how she was not quite twenty and engaged to marry her college boyfriend. How could I ask her to take on such a big responsibility?

When it came time to head north for Connie's wedding, we suggested to our three Brandeis-bound students that they join us and that we could help them settle in with friends of ours until the dorms opened for the summer session. With Joe Leggett along for the trip as well, we had six people crammed into the car as we drove to Memphis to catch our plane. We stayed that first night in a motel near the airport and went to see the new musical *Finian's Rainbow*, a political satire in which a bigoted white politician magically turns black. Times were changing quickly in Memphis. Nobody looked twice at our integrated group as we walked into the movie theater, a white family with a black teenager. And no one stopped us when we all sat on the main floor, ignoring the black balcony.

I found myself lost in thought for the entire flight back to Boston. Why wasn't I more excited about returning? Slowly, the truth dawned on me. I no longer belonged in the Northeast; I had moved on. We all had. Of course it would be good to see our family and friends, but it would also be good to return to Mound Bayou. Had it, despite all the difficulties, become our home?

During the remainder of that summer, I thought often of our visit north and my reactions to it. We'd come to take for granted our frugal lifestyle in Mound Bayou, forgetting the luxury of the life we had known in Boston. It was eye-opening to experience that opulence once again and realize how awkward it made us feel. When we lived in Newton we viewed ourselves as middle-class, struggling to keep up financially as Leon built his practice and we paid off all the bills from medical school. Although we'd given lip service to recognizing that most of the world would consider us wealthy, it wasn't until we moved to Mississippi that we recognized how well off we'd been all those years, and how few people were that fortunate.

We had been both affluent and happy in our former lives; in Mound Bayou, while we no longer enjoyed the benefits of that affluence, we were still happy. I did miss my friends and family, but I didn't miss the luxuries. More than that, it felt good to be part of something important. Despite my happiness, however, without school to keep me busy over the summer, I was lonely. Leon worked long hours at the clinic, and Philip and Jo were rarely home. Charles and I spent many hours reading together, and I listened while he practiced the piano, yet the time dragged.

I was thus delighted when the news broke that we were to have a new community center with a man-made lake, provided compliments of Bolivar County. Just as it had several years earlier when the citizens of Cleveland had built a pool for Mound Bayou to keep blacks out of their whites-only pool, the white citizens' prejudice worked to our advantage. The county had approved an elaborate park for the residents of Cleveland and decided it had to create a similar recreational space near Mound Bayou.

The lake offered some relief from the boredom of the long summer days. I'd always loved swimming, and it was a wonderful way to pass the time, once I got myself there. Spending time on the shore with the school librarian, Mary Gates, made me realize just how lonely I was. Although my colleagues at school in general seemed to accept me, they never invited me to join them on our days off, other than to go to church. Scared that I'd be imposing, I didn't invite them either.

But it was comfortable when I found Mary at the lake. I'd spread my towel near her without even realizing, and she just started chatting, asking me how my summer was going. How I appreciated her reaching out to me like that! We talked of the upcoming school year and wondered how the students at Brandeis were doing. She asked about Connie's wedding, and I shared with her how odd it had made me feel to be back in Boston. After lounging in the sun together for almost an hour, I took the plunge and asked her a question that I hoped she wouldn't view as too forward.

"I've been curious about something ever since this

beach opened up. I lie in the sun to get a tan. But you can't tan. Doesn't that make this seem like a waste of time?"

She laughed. "What a funny thought!" she said. "I love the feeling of the sun on my face and the warmth and the breeze. It doesn't matter at all that I don't tan." Then she laughed again. "But I sure can get burned if I stay out here too long, just like you. We better head back home."

August 1968
Jo (11 years old)

I turned eleven this summer and got my first taste of total independence. Nobody pays attention to me, so I've been able to do whatever I want. I got to ride bareback on a horse that was a little bit wild and I didn't complain when it tossed me in the ditch by the side of the road. I went fishing in a creek and almost stepped on a water moccasin. I even hitchhiked out to the new lake, letting my parents believe that I was catching a ride with friends.

Every morning, I go out and find Clarence, Toda-Jack, and Flit. Sometimes we shoot baskets or throw a baseball around. We spend hours up in a tree house that some older guys built in a tree in the middle of the overgrown field behind our trailers.

I had a great time at the lake the first few times I went, but then I stopped going because whenever I'd swim more than a few feet from the shore, some boy would try to put his hand inside my bathing suit. I never learned whether it was one boy doing it all the time or several boys, but it happened even when I went with my family and my mother was only twenty feet away. One time it happened when Charles was swimming right next to me. I don't know whether he didn't notice or was too embarrassed to say anything.

Fall 1968
Aura (46 years old)

While I waited for the fall to arrive, I played the piano. I did needlework. I wrote letters. Still, the time passed slowly. I needed something to challenge my intellect, the way the summer courses at Brandeis had done. It was too late to look into summer school, but it dawned on me that I could be a student again come fall. Delta State College was only eight miles away, in Cleveland. I was sure they'd have a program through which I could earn a teaching certificate.

Wasting no time, I called the education department head to schedule an appointment to discuss the possibilities. The secretary asked for my name, address, and phone number and said someone would get back to me. Several days later, I hadn't heard from anyone, so I called again.

"I don't mean to be a bother," I said, "but the semester is starting in a couple of weeks and I don't want to miss the registration deadline. Is there any way I can get in to see the dean?"

"He is unavailable at this time," his secretary said stiffly. "You'll just have to wait. Someone will return your call."

When another week went by with no response, I tried once again. This time, she was downright brusque. I got the impression that she hadn't even passed on my requests to the dean. "Tomorrow's the deadline. If you won't give me an appointment immediately, I'll just have to show up and wait in the office."

Clearly disturbed by this possibility, she reluctantly gave me an appointment for the next day. I drove to Cleveland filled with excitement. My mood soared as I found the education department and introduced myself. The secretary pointed me toward her boss's office. There I found a middle-aged man sitting behind his desk with his feet up, staring down at a paper. I stood there waiting. He ignored me, refusing to acknowledge my presence. After what seemed like a very long time, I cleared my throat to get his attention. He looked up. When he saw me, he rose quickly, came around the desk, noticeably flustered, and led me to a chair, saying, "I beg your pardon. I thought you were . . ."

I suddenly knew what he was going to say; the look on his face made it obvious. Now I understood why he hadn't called me back and had been so rude when I first entered his office. His secretary had assumed from my address that I was black. I hadn't realized it, but Delta State College, though bound by law to accept black students, was still an all-white institution.

I hesitated, unsure how to proceed. I wanted to take a class, but how could I attend a segregated school? I thought about my difficulties in our early days in Mound Bayou, when I'd felt ostracized for having used a whites-only bathroom, and worried that going to Delta State would rekindle those hostilities. I hardly noticed the dean explaining my course options as I felt my dream falling apart. What had started as an exciting idea had become a strong desire. I desperately wanted to take graduate classes at Delta State, despite its unwillingness to accept black students. Ignoring the dean's words, I silently jumped through mental hoops, trying to justify the action

I wanted to take. Learning about theories of education would make me a better teacher and would thus help my students. Everyone in Mound Bayou would see it that way, wouldn't they? Our family had proven time and time again that we weren't like the racist citizens of Cleveland. Surely nobody would hold it against me if I took advantage of this opportunity to improve myself.

Unwilling to give up my dream, I buried my sense of guilt and focused instead on the dean. He said I could begin class the following week and would be able to attend in the late afternoon so it wouldn't interfere with my teaching. Driving home, I alternated between being on top of the world and feeling terribly guilty for having rationalized away my taking advantage of white privilege.

TEN

❧

DREAMING *the* IMPOSSIBLE

Every great dream begins with a dreamer. Always remember, you have within you the strength, the patience, and the passion to reach for the stars to change the world.

—HARRIET TUBMAN, 1820—1913

Fall 1968
Aura (46 years old)

M y Adolescent Psychology class at Delta State was
fantastic. Every day we discussed what goes on in
the mind of a teenager. All the other students could draw
only on their personal experiences of adolescence,
whereas I had the added perspective of parenting my own
teenage children and a year of working with my students.

One conversation revolved around how much freedom
parents should give their teenagers in selecting a college.
Some students believed that eighteen was old enough to
make important life decisions. Others said the parents
were entitled to choose because they were footing the bill.
One young man repeated what his father had said: "If your
feet are under my table, I have the right to make decisions
for you."

Eventually, several students asked me what I thought.

"If your feet are under my table, I have the right to see
that you are well fed," I said.

They all laughed, but then one student said, "What
does that mean?"

"Of course I have to make the decisions when it comes
to critical issues, like the safety of my children. But when
it comes to how they should dress or how long they
should wear their hair or even where they should go to
school, my children have to decide that for themselves.
How will they learn how to be adults if I decide for
them?"

One young man called out, "My father would probably
disown me if I said something like that to him."

Often, my comments included anecdotes about my experiences with my students in Mound Bayou. I made no secret of the fact that I lived and worked in an all-black town. One morning, a young lady walked up to me after class and asked to speak to me for a few minutes. "You need to be more careful about what you say in class," she said. "Some of the students belong to the Ku Klux Klan and the White Citizens' Council, and they're not happy with all your talk about Mound Bayou."

"What would you have me do? Should I hide who I am and what I do?" I asked, my tone making it clear that I had no intention of doing any such thing.

"This is serious, Mrs. Kruger. You could be in danger."

"I'm sure you're exaggerating. We're all friends in there."

"It may seem like that to you, but I hear some of them talking after class. They may seem polite and respectful, but you're a threat to them."

"Me? I'm just trying to help."

"That's not what I mean. You're like the carpetbaggers after the Civil War. You want them to change who they are and what they believe."

"You're right. If they believe that it's acceptable to make black people live as second-class citizens, then they need to change."

"I don't disagree with you, but many of them do. Just be careful, please. You really could be in danger. People have been beaten up for saying the kinds of things you say."

I thanked her for the warning but told her I had no choice. "Somebody's got to make them think. If I don't do it, who will?"

After we talked for several more minutes, I invited her to come home with me for lunch to continue our conversation. She said, "I'd love to come, Mrs. Kruger, but I'm kind of scared. I've never been in a black neighborhood, let alone a black town."

"That can't be true."

"The only black person I've ever spoken with is our maid."

"Come to my home. It'll be just the two of us. You won't have to talk with anyone else."

"Are you sure it's safe?"

"You'll be fine," I reassured her. "You can follow close behind me in your car and park right in my front yard. Everyone will know you're with me."

"I don't know . . ."

"You won't regret it. I promise you'll be safe." As I spoke those words, I suddenly had a sick feeling in the pit of my stomach. What if they weren't true? What if something happened like when our home was stoned? Pushing my fear away, I repeated my invitation one last time, not really expecting her to accept. She did.

Knowing that many in the white community viewed us as low-class trash for our involvement in Mound Bayou, I set an elaborate table using bone china, crystal, and sterling silver, and the results were as elegant as anything you'd find in the richest mansion in the state. Although I personally didn't value such displays anymore, I knew my guest had been brought up to do so, and it made it easier for her to respect me and listen to what I had to say.

Over the meal, she told me more about herself, beginning with the fact that she was Senator Eastland's niece. No wonder she was afraid to come to Mound Bayou!

She'd grown up in a family that was terrified of blacks and believed they should be kept completely separate from white society. Her uncle was the state's foremost spokesman for segregation, quoted on National Public Radio for his comments when addressing a meeting of the White Citizens' Council: "When in the course of human events it becomes necessary to abolish the Negro race, proper methods should be used. Among these are guns, bows and arrows, slingshots, and knives." It was the same kind of attitude that led to the extermination of Jews in Germany.

While I was reflecting on what my young guest's uncle would think about me—a Jewish Northerner helping the black community—she brought me back to the present as if she had read my mind, saying, "My uncle would have a fit if he knew I was here."

"You should tell him," I said, "and maybe you'll be able to influence him to change."

"It's hopeless. I know his attitude is wrong, but I'm not like you. I can't just defy him the way you do. My whole family thinks the way he does. They'd never speak to me again if I even told them I'd been here with you."

By the end of our meal, however, she said, "Maybe you're right. Maybe one day I'll light my own little candle."

Jo (11 years old)

Mom likes her new school. And Philip likes his high school in Amherst. Now that I've transferred to seventh grade at the public school, I'm happy too. But I sure wasn't before. I was miserable in the sixth grade at St. Gabriel's. I didn't like my teacher. She was a lot stricter than Sister Anne was last year. And she wanted me to cross myself and pretend to be Christian, only she didn't call it pretending. She said that Judaism was just another denomination of Christianity and that I was spoiled for thinking that I was different from the other kids. She got mad when I said that reading Bible stories in history class wasn't really studying history.

And I didn't like being in the same class as Charles. Because sixth and seventh grade were combined in one room, we were together. He always seemed to understand the readings quicker than me and he sometimes teased me about it. To tell the truth, though, what I really wanted was to transfer to the public school as an excuse to skip a grade. That's what Philip did. Mom and Dad wouldn't let me switch just to go up a grade, so I told them that I was unhappy about the religious stuff. It wasn't a lie; it just wasn't the whole truth. I feel kind of guilty about it, but I'm sure glad I did it.

Today was my first day, and it was pretty good. We have different teachers for every class, and I get to play my flute in the band. If I'm good enough, they'll let me be in the marching band, but that probably won't happen for a couple of years. They don't usually let kids in until high school. I miss being in the school orchestra at my old school in Newton, and nobody here is really helping me get any better on the flute, but I'll just keep practicing and see what happens. One good thing about the new school is that I'll see more of my friends. I had friends at the Catholic school, but my best friends are Clarence, Toda-Jack, and Flit, and they're all at the public school.

My math class was strange. The teacher showed us how to do long division, which I'd already learned how to do in fourth grade in Newton, but he didn't do it right. He said to ignore all zeros in the answer. I raised my hand and said, "You can't do that. You have to keep the zeros."

Mr. Brown glared at me and then turned back to the board. I didn't know what to do. I was sure he was wrong. Mom and Dad had warned me that the school wouldn't be as good as St. Gabriel's, but this was pretty amazing. How could he not know how to divide? And what should I do? I was torn. I didn't want to make him look bad in front of the class, but, if I'm honest about it, I wanted to show off that I knew more than he did. So I repeated myself.

After looking at it again, he grumbled and changed what he'd written, and I thought that was the end of it. But I was wrong. After dinner that night, he showed up at our trailer to talk with my parents. I was scared that he was going to tell them I couldn't stay at the school, that he didn't want me in his class. I guess I couldn't blame him. I'd shown him up in front of all those kids, and he must have been really mad at me. So when they sat down to talk at the dining room table, I sat on the floor in the hall and eavesdropped, my stomach all tight at the thought of how mad my folks were going to be.

Aura (46 years old)

It's not the food that made dinnertime special. It was the conversation. Not a night went by that we didn't hear from the children about their day at school or out and about in the neighborhood. Leon told us about his day at the clinic, and I told everyone what happened in my class. We talked about the books the children were reading or our plans for our next trip to Memphis.

One night, the conversation focused on Jo's first day at

the public school. She seemed quite happy with the transition. She already knew a lot of her classmates, and she really liked that they had a band and she got to switch rooms every period. Her social studies teacher pulled her aside and said that he was going to make sure she was challenged in his class, so she would have to do some extra-credit reports. Other students might have grumbled at being singled out for additional work, but not Jo. She looked forward to pulling out the encyclopedia later that evening and starting her research.

I had just finished clearing the table, and Leon and I were about to wash the dishes, when we heard someone at the front door. Visitors were unusual, as most of our friends were uneasy about entering a white person's home. A quiet young man—dressed in a black Sunday suit, complete with a thin black tie and a hat—greeted me at the door and introduced himself as Jo's new math teacher. He cleared his throat several times and was clearly uncomfortable. Thinking that perhaps he was going to suggest additional work for Jo in math, just as her social studies teacher had done, I invited him in for coffee and we settled around the dining room table.

He looked about the room nervously, his fingers tapping on the table. We waited, figuring he'd speak when he was ready. Then he took a deep breath, as if preparing himself for a difficult task.

"I want to apologize for what happened in class today," he said, looking down at the hat he held in his lap.

"What are you talking about? Jo didn't say anything about any problem," I said, smiling encouragement yet curious to know what had happened.

"I'm supposed to be teaching shop. But the school

doesn't have a math teacher, so I'm doing the best I can."

Leon, who at one time dreamed of being a math teacher, perked up. "What happened?" he asked.

"I'm surprised Jo didn't tell you. I was trying to teach the class how to divide, but I got it all wrong. If she hadn't corrected me, the rest of the class would never have known the difference. Later on in school, they'd make the same mistake I made and people would think they were stupid. And it would all be my fault."

He never looked up as he spoke, ashamed of his lack of knowledge. Then, feeling a need to explain further, he added, "I know I'm not very good at teaching math, but I'm the best they've got. If I don't teach it, they won't have a math class." Then, for the first time since we'd sat down at the table, he stared directly at Leon. "What else can I do? I'm really sorry that I can't do any better. Your little girl deserves a good math teacher. So do all the students."

We didn't know what to say. We couldn't just say that it was okay, because it wasn't. He was right. All we could do was thank him for taking the time to tell us what was going on. And I worried about my students who were now at Brandeis; I wondered how they were getting on and whether they were woefully unprepared to deal with the academic environment I'd encouraged them to embrace.

After he left, Leon said, "I'm going to start a remedial math class for adults in the evening."

"Maybe Father Guidry will let you use a classroom at St. Gabriel's," I said. "I can ask him, if you like."

Within a few days of that conversation, I was no longer the only teacher in our household. It meant even less time for the two of us to spend together, but I found it gratifying nevertheless.

୬

THE SCHOOL TERM ENDED, the holidays passed, and the spring semester got under way. All over the country, people who'd been deeply disturbed by the assassination of Martin Luther King Jr. the previous spring spoke of celebrating his birthday on January 15. Initially, my students proposed boycotting their classes, saying that's what Dr. King would have wanted them to do. I countered that they should stay in school, reminding them that Dr. King valued education so much that he had written about its power back in 1947, while still a student at Morehouse College. There he penned his paper "The Purpose of Education," in which he said, "Education must enable a man to achieve . . . the goals of his life." Responding to my urging them to stay in school, they asked the principal to allow them to conduct a memorial assembly, much as we'd done the spring before.

The students used my classroom as their base of operations, planning the program, selecting literature and political quotes to read aloud, drawing from material we'd been studying all year. They stood in front of my bulletin boards, rereading the numerous articles, stories, and poems I'd been posting since the day I arrived—quotes from Dr. King, Eldridge Cleaver, and Malcolm X; poems by Langston Hughes; articles I'd read out loud to them; slogans such as "Black Pride" and "Black is beautiful"; and news clippings about the Black Panthers.

Most people—even many blacks—thought of the Panthers as a violent organization, one to be feared. But I told my students the complete story, starting with its founding in 1966, its original purpose having been to fight police brutality in the black ghetto. As the organization spread across the country, it began to help in other ways as well, arranging for free breakfasts for schoolchildren and free medical clinics for those who were sick or injured. They helped the homeless find housing and gave away clothing and food.

While some students prepared a talk about the Black Panthers, another one rehearsed a reading from the Langston Hughes poem suite *Montage of a Dream Deferred*: "What happens to a dream deferred? / Does it dry up like a raisin in the sun? . . . / Maybe it just sags like a heavy load. / Or does it explode?" As I listened, it occurred to me that I was helping my classes to know they had the right to dream, and that what they learned in my class would help them achieve their dreams.

By the end of the planning and the event, I felt even closer to my students than I had before. Apparently, they felt close to me as well, for, a few days later, I found a note on my desk saying, *Mrs. Kruger, you are now an honorary Black Panther.* It was a label I wore with pride.

Jo (11 years old)

I was falling asleep in my English class. It was hot and stuffy, and we were listening to *Romeo and Juliet* on a record. This was the third day of doing nothing but sitting around. Stifling a yawn, I stared at the clock over the teacher's desk, willing it to move faster. Five more minutes until the bell signaling our morning break, when we could go out to the schoolyard and get the popcorn they sold at a stand for a nickel. I let myself buy it only once or twice a week, or it would use up all my allowance.

Finally! We all jumped up, ignoring our teacher as she tried to tell us what we'd be doing tomorrow, her voice lost in the scuff of chairs scratching along the floor and the jibber jabber of our voices. Everyone wanted to be at the front of the line for popcorn so we could finish eating before our next class started. A lot of the teachers made you throw away anything that was left before you could sit down.

My third-period teacher, Mr. Henry, wouldn't even let us do that. He said he didn't want our garbage in his trashcan, and so we couldn't even bring it into his room. He said he was tired of all the popcorn on the floor and made it against the rules. At first nobody listened to him and brought it in anyway. It was easy to ignore his rules because he was usually so easygoing. Tall and gaunt, with a trim mustache, he had a friendly smile and seemed to really want us to learn about the history of art. That's what he taught. My folks were surprised when I told them about the class, and they kept telling me how lucky I was, that it wasn't even offered at Weeks Junior High back in Newton.

Eventually, Mr. Henry got so frustrated with the mess that he said the next student to bring popcorn into the class was going to regret it. I wasn't sure what he meant by that, but I could guess. In Newton, the teachers weren't allowed to hit the students, but it happened pretty often in Mound Bayou. When I was at St. Gabriel's, the sisters would rap students on their hands to keep them quiet. It never happened to me, but it looked painful. Last year, when Philip was still in town, he spoke up against corporal punishment and got suspended for a couple of days when he refused to be hit.

I'd been watching for an opportunity to do the same. It was pretty cool the way Philip was willing to protest what he thought was wrong, and I wanted to be like him and make a statement as well. So when Mr. Henry got mad at the whole class because he found popcorn on the floor one more time, I was ready.

"Who did it?" he asked, knowing that we knew exactly what he was talking about. Then he picked up a leather strap he kept hanging on a nail behind his desk. "If nobody tells me who dropped that popcorn, I'm going to whip the whole class."

Everyone kept quiet. There was no way he'd go through with his threat.

"Last chance," he said, flipping the strap against his hand over and over again.

Finally, one boy spoke up. "It wasn't none of us."

"Oh, really?"

"Yessuh. It was some boy in here during the break."

"Did he have a name? No? Okay, then. Everybody line up."

"What's happening?" I whispered to the girl sitting next to me as everyone started to stand up.

"No big deal," she answered. "The boys'll get hit on their behinds, but he'll just kind of tap the girls on their hands."

This was my chance. I could be a hero and make Mr. Henry back down. Jostling my way to the front of the line, I just stood there looking at him, not sure what to do next.

"Well?" he asked, waiting for me to hold out my hand.

"I won't be hit," I mumbled.

"What was that?"

"I refuse to be hit." For the first time, I felt scared. Was he going to hit me anyway? I suddenly realized that I had no idea what Philip had actually done, how he had handled things.

It seemed like forever before Mr. Henry said, "Get out of here." Just like that, I was suspended. I hadn't accomplished anything. I hadn't stopped him from hitting everyone. He was already looking past me to the next kid in line.

"Where do I go?"

"I don't really care," he answered coldly. "Just get out of my classroom."

I walked slowly back to my desk to gather up my books. I tried again to ask what I should do, but he interrupted, raising his voice for the first time, and shouted, "Go!"

When I'd started this, it had felt kind of like a game. I hadn't meant to make Mr. Henry mad; I'd just wanted to do something important. But now I could feel my eyes starting to tear up, and I dashed out of the room before anybody could see. Then I ran down the hallway toward the exit and almost crashed into Principal Gates before I stopped.

"Whoa!" he said. "Slow down." He started to reach for me but then let his hand drop to his side. "What's going on?"

At first, still in a daze, I couldn't say anything. When I found my voice, all I could do was stutter. "I-I . . ."

"Take a breath, Jo, and tell me what happened."

He listened patiently and then said, "Well, you can't go home."

At first I thought he was saying that I wasn't suspended. How was I going to make my political statement if he just made me go to class?

"I can't go back in. Mr. Henry won't let me."

"No, I suppose that's true. What shall we do with you?"

Why was he asking me? I didn't know. I shrugged my shoulders.

"How about if we walk over to the high school and ask your mother?"

I felt relieved. She would take over. And she'd be proud of me for taking a stand about corporal punishment.

⚘

IT DIDN'T TAKE LONG for Mr. Gates and my mother to decide I would sit in the back of her classroom for a week. Now I couldn't believe what I was seeing. The chalkboard was covered with all these nasty comments about Jews. My mother had underlined the word "Jews" in big letters right in the middle. Then, scattered all about, she was writing what the students called out: "greedy and money-hungry," "ugly with big noses," "killed our savior." And they were still going. "Horns," one called out. My mother put it up on the board.

"Anything else?" she asked.

"They be prejudiced against blacks."

How could her students say all these nasty things about Jews? Didn't they know we're Jewish? Did they really think that we're prejudiced? I remembered last Easter, when I was still at the Catholic school, and a friend said that I killed Jesus. I didn't even know what he was talking about. He told me that the Bible said the Jews murdered the son of God. When I told him that I didn't have anything to do with that, he just shrugged it off. Then we talked about shooting baskets at recess.

But this was different. My mother was actually encouraging the students to think about every bad thing they'd ever heard about Jews. "Funny accents." Up it went on the board. "Kikes." There was no way she would write that one. We weren't allowed to say it at home; it was as bad as the N-word. But she wrote it as if it were the easiest thing in the world.

"How many of you have ever met a Jew?"

I almost raised my hand, forgetting I didn't really belong there. "Anyone?"

"No, but I'd know one if I saw one."

"Really. And do you really know what Jews are like?"

Some nodded. Others shook their heads.

"Do I have a big, ugly nose and horns?"

"No, ma'am."

"Have you forgotten that I'm Jewish?" she asked quietly.

"But you're not like the Jews around here."

"How can you know that?"

Silence. "Anyone?"

There was some awkward coughing. Some students stared out the window. Others looked down at their desks. One boy kept tapping the desk with his pencil, and it sounded really loud.

"Now you're ready to read Shakespeare's *The Merchant of Venice.*" So that's what she was doing. We'd read it at home over the summer, taking turns reading parts out loud. I couldn't understand everything, but I remembered that there was a Jewish man named Shylock who loaned some money to a Christian merchant, even though the merchant hated him and made fun of him for being Jewish. She had told us that even though the played was called *The Merchant of Venice*, it could just as well have been called *The Tragedy of Shylock* and was about anti-Semitism.

I waited for her to erase all the nasty things she'd written on the board, but she didn't, even when some of the students asked her to. Instead, she assigned roles and had everyone start reading out loud. It was just as boring as listening to the record of *Romeo and Juliet* in my own English class, and I found it hard to stay awake.

Things got exciting, though, when they got to Shylock's answer when the merchant asks him for a loan. She stopped the student who was reading and said, "I'm going to read this next speech for you, to make it easier to understand." And she did. Everyone listened quietly as she did her best portrayal of Shylock. But when she asked what she had just said, nobody tried to answer.

"Come on, now. I know you can get this. Listen again to the first line: *You call me misbeliever, cutthroat dog . . .*"

"He's complaining that the merchant calls him names."

"That's right. What kind of names?"

"Misbeliever."

"Okay. So he doesn't believe what the Christians believe."

"And he calls him a dog."

"Right." Then my mom went up to the board where she'd written all the mean things the students had said earlier and added the word "dog" to the list. "Now listen to the next line: *And spit upon my Jewish gabardine . . .*"

"Here's a new vocabulary word. Does anybody know what 'gabardine' means? No? I'll help. It's a kind of cloth. In Shakespeare's day, it might have been a cloak."

"So the Christians spit on his clothes?"

"Yes. They call him a dog and spit on him."

"That's just not right, Miz Kruger."

"Listen again to the end of the speech:
Shall I bend low, with whispering humbleness, Say this;
'Fair sir, you spit on me on Wednesday last;
You spurn'd me such a day; another time
You call'd me dog; and for these courtesies
I'll lend you thus much moneys'?"

By the end of it, she sounded all choked up like she was going to cry. I looked around, and everyone was staring at her. She waited quietly, breathing deeply as if to calm herself. "What would you do if you were Shylock?"

"No way I'd be loaning the money," said one student.

"He's evil, Miz Kruger," said another. "It'd be like the KKK comin' into town and telling us we should be helping them out."

"Does everyone else feel the same way?" Most of the students nodded. "Good. Your homework for tonight is to write a paragraph about how you'd feel if someone treated you like you're dirt and then asked you for a favor. What would you do?"

THE NEXT DAY, we finished reading the scene. Again, my mother read Shylock's lines when she wanted the students to really pay attention:

"I am a Jew. . . . If you prick us, do we not bleed? If you tickle us, do we not laugh? If you poison us, do we not die? And if you wrong us, shall we not revenge?"

By this time, it seemed as if everyone understood without her having to go back and explain. They all were listening closely, and then she repeated those lines, substituting the words "I am a woman" for "I am a Jew." I looked around, and most of the girls were nodding. Then everyone laughed when one girl rapped the boy in front of her on the head, saying, "That's right."

Once the laughter died down, my mother started up again, this time saying, "I am black. If you prick us, do we not bleed?"

"No way, Miz Kruger. Shakespeare never wrote that, did he?"

"No, but he could have. He was dealing with issues three hundred years ago that are still with us today. What was Shylock saying to the merchant?"

"'I'm a person, just like you.'"

"And is there anyone you might like to tell that to?"

"My parents," said one student.

"That's what the Black Panthers be sayin' to white people, isn't it?" asked another.

"We want respect!"

Then one of the girls sang the first line of "Respect," kind of dancing in her seat. Everyone laughed, and one student called out, "That's right, girl." My mother walked over to the bulletin board and patted a picture of Aretha Franklin she'd posted there, from the cover of *TIME* magazine.

"That's your assignment for tonight. I want you to write about what it feels like to not be respected, whether it's because you're young, or female, or black, or anything else you want to write about."

⟡

LATER IN THE WEEK, the classroom discussion turned toward Jessica, Shylock's daughter, who fell in love with a Christian named Lorenzo. After explaining that Jessica plans on marrying him and converting, my mother read the lines, "*Alack, what heinous sin is it in me / To be ashamed to be my father's child!*"

"Why is she ashamed?" my mother asked.

"Because she thinks her father is mean?" one student responded.

"What makes you think he's mean? He's making the loan to the merchant, right?"

"I guess. He just doesn't seem very nice."

"Anybody else? No? Let's look at the rest of the speech:
*But though I am a daughter to his blood,
I am not to his manners. O Lorenzo,
If thou keep promise, I shall end this strife,
Become a Christian and thy loving wife.*

"What is Jessica saying here?"

"She's not like Shylock."

"And she's going to become Christian."

"Right. Now, Shakespeare isn't here to tell us exactly what he meant by these lines, so all we can do is make our best guess. But traditionally these lines have been interpreted to mean that Jessica's ashamed of being Jewish. How do you think you would feel if you felt that way about your background?"

"Miz Kruger, is it all right if I hate being black?"

"That jes be wrong, sister. I'm black and I'm proud!"

I glanced at the bulletin board at the picture of the James Brown album that had just been released last year.

"That's right. Say it loud!"

Then everyone seemed to join in, jumping all over the girl who had said she hated being black. It took my mom a few moments to get everyone to quiet down.

"All your lives, you've been hearing people saying nasty things about blacks, just like Jessica heard mean things about Jews." She walked over to the board and added, "I'm not going to ask you what a group of white students from Shelby might have said if I'd asked them to tell me what they know about blacks, but it would probably be just as bad, if not worse."

"Can't you erase that, Miz Kruger?"

"Okay. It's time." You could feel the sense of relief as she wiped the board clean. The class had clearly become embarrassed by what they had said on that first day.

"Tonight's assignment? I want you to listen to the James Brown song, 'Say It Loud'" she said, tapping the picture of the album, "and write about how it makes you feel."

Aura (46 years old)

Everything was going so well for our family that we just assumed we'd stay in Mound Bayou well beyond our original two-year commitment. Philip was flourishing at his school in Amherst, so we stopped worrying about our children's education and assumed that, if necessary, Charles and Jo could follow in his footsteps. Our trailer had become as much of a home to us as our house in

Boston had been. Leon still had many improvements he wanted to implement at the clinic, and I still had much more I wanted to teach my students in the classroom. We were thus crestfallen when Leon's boss pointed out that it was time for Leon to start looking for work elsewhere. Leon told Jack that he wanted to stay, that the family had settled into our life there and had no desire to return to Boston, even though the two years were coming to an end. But Jack was insistent, reminding Leon of their desire to turn over the management of the clinic to the black community. The other white pediatrician had left with his family after just one year, and now, whether we wanted to or not, it was our turn to leave as well.

Determined to make our last few months important, Leon tackled his innovations at the clinic with renewed enthusiasm, and I realized that the time had come for me to figure out what to do with the $1,000 that the family of one of Leon's patients in Boston had given us. It had happened over the summer, when we were visiting. Leon had called on the family to see how the child was doing, concerned because the boy had been in a coma until just before we'd left for Mound Bayou. Grateful for Leon's efforts in keeping their son alive, the parents offered an extra payment. When Leon refused, the father said, "Keep it. If you won't take it for yourself, use it for the people in Mississippi."

After several evenings of brainstorming with Leon over the dinner table, I decided to buy classroom sets of four paperback books: *Where Do We Go from Here: Chaos or Community?*, by Dr. Martin Luther King Jr.; *The Autobiography of Malcolm X*, as told to Alex Haley; Shakespeare's *Othello*; and an anthology called *Currents in Poetry*. Leon added that we should then donate the remainder of the money to Father Guidry to help students at the Catholic school.

When I'd started teaching eighteen months earlier, I'd kept looking to my principal to give me guidance regarding what to teach. I had never gotten any. No matter what I'd said, Mr. Moore had told me it was perfect, so I'd grown accustomed to just doing whatever I wanted in the classroom. It thus never occurred to me to seek approval before buying new books. I was completely in charge of my classroom, and we'd been discussing both Dr. King and Malcolm X for over a year without anyone's objecting. But when word of the books' arrival spread, it set off a firestorm in the community. How dare I bring such incendiary material into the classroom? Before I had a chance to take the books from their boxes, Mr. Jones, the superintendent, called me to his office at the high school and said, "Mrs. Kruger, you can't use them."

I stuttered for a moment, struggling to understand what was happening. "Why not?" I asked, trying to keep from sounding upset.

"You know how people are objecting. Do you have any idea how many phone calls I've gotten from upset parents?"

"I-I didn't realize . . ."

"They're very upset. You've opened quite a can of worms."

"What do they find objectionable? Is it anything in particular?"

"It's the whole idea of the books."

"But I've been talking with my students all year about black literature," I said slowly. "Nobody has complained before. Why is it different now?"

"It just is. Parents don't want their children getting into any trouble. Nobody wants to make waves."

"Have they even read the books?"

"That doesn't matter."

"Of course it matters. How can you cave in to their demands if they don't know what's in the books?"

"It's not that simple."

"What do you think, Mr. Jones?" I asked. "Don't you think we should expose our students to the actual writings of these men about whom they've heard so much?"

Without a moment's hesitation, he answered, "No. If you hand out those books to your students, the KKK will hear about it and take action. They might even burn down the town. We can't afford to risk it."

I went home that evening feeling disturbed and confused. Leon and I discussed my dilemma over dinner, and he promised to seek advice from his colleagues at the clinic. The next night, he told me that they had suggested I speak with Aaron Henry, president of the Mississippi chapter of the NAACP.

I'd heard many good things about Mr. Henry, known nationally for bringing an integrated delegation to the 1964 Democratic National Convention and demanding to be let in. He'd said his group of delegates was more representative of Mississippi than the all-white one the state party had sent. Eventually, both delegations had been allowed in as a compromise. Given his extensive experience fighting for civil rights and the successes he'd achieved, I was both nervous and thrilled at the prospect of meeting him.

I called Mr. Henry the following day, and he agreed to meet with Leon and me. We drove the forty miles north to Clarksdale to see him at his drugstore. The three of us sat down at a table, and I described my situation. "Do you think it's appropriate for me to bring these books into my classroom?"

"Absolutely," he said. "Why do you doubt yourself?"

"It's hard not to, when I find myself fighting against blacks."

"Welcome to the club."

"Wh—"

"I've been doing that for years."

I listened in amazement as he told me that for many years, he'd battled other blacks in his efforts to bring the civil rights movement to Mississippi. Mr. Henry was all too familiar with my plight and assured me I was on the right track, difficult as it was. "Please don't give up, Mrs. Kruger. Your students and the townspeople need you, whether they know it or not."

When I asked for some practical suggestions regarding how to proceed, he said, "I want you to call on Dr. Burton. He knows all about Mound Bayou and will know how to handle things."

I knew Dr. Burton's name but had never met the man. Before he'd retired, he had run the old Taborian Hospital and hadn't especially welcomed Leon's new clinic. I looked to Leon for guidance, but he just waited for me to take the lead.

"I'm not sure how to approach him, Mr. Henry. He's got a reputation for being somewhat standoffish, and I'm not sure he'd be willing to talk with me."

"I'm sure he will. He's been an ardent civil rights advocate for a long time. You go back to town and look him up." I promised I'd call Dr. Burton when I got home, and we said good-bye.

As it turned out, Leon and I both had important calls to make. Shortly after I spoke with Dr. Burton and arranged to visit with him, Leon called the University of Miami about the possibility of setting up a clinic in Liberty City, Miami's black inner city. We'd heard about riots there the previous summer and knew the community could benefit from a clinic like the one Leon had built in Mound Bayou, but it hadn't occurred to Leon to seek work there until Jack had told him that he'd be out of a job in June. The university was intrigued with Leon's call and asked him to come to Miami for an interview.

Miami! Much as I wanted to stay in Mound Bayou and continue the work I'd started with my students, I was happy about the thought of living in Florida. Not only did I love the beauty of the place, but also my parents had settled there when we'd left Boston for Mississippi. I thought this might discourage Leon from moving there, for although I was almost fifty years old, I still found it difficult to stand up to my father, and that always annoyed Leon. But it had been years since Leon had complained about my father's hold over me, so it was easy for me to assume that it no longer bothered him. I grew even less anxious about the issue when Leon actually said that it would be nice for us to reunite with my parents.

I wholeheartedly agreed. For the first time in two years, I would have family close by. I had colleagues in Mound Bayou, but, with the exception of Pauline and Preston Holmes, I had nobody with whom I could truly relax. I always had to be on my guard, careful lest something I say be interpreted the wrong way. And I couldn't talk about my children with anyone, for fear that people would consider it bragging.

Although I was already looking forward in some ways to moving to Miami and hoped that Leon's trip there would prove fruitful, I had much work left to do in Mound Bayou. So I wished him luck on his interviews and he wished me luck on my upcoming discussion with Dr. Burton. As he drove off to catch his flight, I wished he could be with me for what I hoped would be the grand conclusion of my battle with the school administration, but by now I was accustomed to having to stand on my own. I was ready.

❧

THE FOLLOWING MORNING, I was surprised when my neighbor's younger sister approached me about the meeting. Jackie lived with her brother, Earl, and taught at the high school with me. Despite living next door to each other and working together, we'd not gotten to know each other beyond saying hello when passing in the yard or at school. I was always hesitant to reach out to my colleagues on a personal level; I worried that they'd reject my overtures or, even worse, pretend to welcome me as a friend to avoid offending me, when in reality they wanted nothing to do with me.

Jackie demonstrated that my concerns were unfounded. She had heard about my intention to talk with Dr. Burton and offered to join me. Her willingness to get involved touched me deeply. At the same time, however, I worried about the impact it might have on her.

"Jackie," I said, "I'm not sure that it's a good idea for you to come. This could spiral out of control. It's one thing for me to rock the boat; it's another for you to risk your job over my fight."

"It's not just your fight," she answered. "I appreciate your concern, but what you're trying to do is right. The students need to read those books."

"So long as you know the risks." Then I took her hand in mine to emphasize my words. "It's good to have a friend."

Together, we walked to Dr. Burton's. He listened while I described the situation and told him of my desire to educate my students about civil rights. I explained how I'd bought classroom sets of several books to help in that endeavor, and I choked up when I added that the superintendent had said leaders in our own community were pressuring him to stop me from doing so. I told him what Aaron Henry had said, encouraging me to carry on and telling me that I wasn't alone, that he faced the same sort of opposition.

Dr. Burton completely agreed with Mr. Henry, saying that he'd experienced the same reaction when he'd raised civil rights issues in town. "I'm glad, Mrs. Kruger, that you are willing to speak up. It's important that you do so."

At that point, Jackie spoke for the first time. "I'm embarrassed to admit that until now, I've been unwilling to get involved. But I'm glad I came. Somebody has to do something and not just stand by, letting things continue the way they are."

"So what do we do now?" I asked, after realizing that Jackie had finished her say. "There's a PTA meeting tomorrow night. Do you think that's a good time to raise the issue of the books with the community?"

"It's the perfect opportunity," said Dr. Burton.

"I'll introduce you," added Jackie.

"Be prepared for a lively discussion. There may be very few people willing to risk the wrath of the KKK by bringing inflammatory literature into the classroom."

Before I could protest that this was an unfair description of the books, he held up his hand to stop me. "I know there's a difference between this literature and the revolutionary writings of some of the more extreme figures, but others don't, and they're scared."

We shook hands again at his front door, and he said, "I promise I'll be there."

As we walked home, Jackie said, "I've lived in the same town as Dr. Burton for years, and this was the first time I've ever talked with him. I thought he'd be different, more distant. But he seemed very supportive."

"And so have you, Jackie," I said. "I can't tell you how much it means to me that you were there tonight."

"I didn't really say much."

"That doesn't matter," I answered. "I wish we'd gotten to know each other sooner."

"Me too," she said. "How about if I drive us to the PTA meeting?"

"You don't need to do that. I can drive myself."

"I know I don't need to. I want to. I want everyone to know that I think you should use those books."

I stopped walking and turned to her. "Jackie, you could lose your job. It's one thing if I get fired—we'll get by on Leon's salary—but you're just starting out. If you get fired here, you'll never be able to teach again."

"You don't think I know that? I've been quiet for too long. It's time for me to take a stand."

❧

SOMEHOW, WORD GOT OUT to all my students about what was going on. Before the bell rang for the first period of the day, my students were clamoring to know what I was going to say at the PTA meeting. Nothing makes a teenager want to read something more than having the adults in the community say it's wrong and inappropriate.

"I'm going to tell everyone exactly what I've told you. These are good books, important ones. High school students all over the country are reading them, and you should be given the same opportunity."

"Can we come tonight?" several of them asked.

"I don't see why not," I answered, scrambling internally to think this through. "But mostly you should encourage your parents to come. They should know what's at stake here."

They must have taken me at my word, for when Jackie and I walked into the school gymnatorium later that night, over two hundred parents were there, waiting for the PTA meeting to begin. I recognized several of the town's religious leaders as well. I looked for Dr. Burton in the crowd but didn't see him. I crossed my fingers and hoped he was there.

The chairperson banged his gavel, called for order, had the minutes read, and led the discussion on old business. Caught up in my thoughts about what I would say regarding the books, I found it hard to concentrate on his words and was taken by surprise when he suddenly said, "Since there is no new business, this meeting is closed."

"Excuse me, Mr. Chairman," Jackie called out as she jumped to her feet, "there *is* new business. We want to discuss the books Mrs. Kruger wants to bring into her classroom."

Many called out in agreement, and it took the chairperson a few moments to settle everyone down. Then he said, "School business is not on the agenda for the PTA."

What in the world did he mean by that? Everything the PTA did was school business. I was trying to figure out how to respond to this absurd statement when the room suddenly grew quiet. It took me a moment to realize that Dr. Burton had stood up. Everyone, board members included, waited to hear what he had to say. But as he started to speak, the chairman drowned him out with his gavel. "You are not a member of the PTA. You can't speak here."

Never before had I heard it said that you had to be a member to speak at these meetings. Before I could worry about how to deal with this latest roadblock, Dr. Burton said, "How much does it cost to join?"

"One dollar."

Dr. Burton walked slowly to the front of the room, reached into his pocket, took out a bill, and placed it on the table in front of the chairman. "Now I'm a member," he said. Turning his back to the board, he faced the parents and said, "I wonder how many of you have actually read these books that Mrs. Kruger wishes to introduce into her classroom. I want you to give her a chance to tell you why she thinks they're important."

Not waiting for approval from the chair, he gestured for me to stand and speak my mind. "Thank you, Dr. Burton . . ." I started to say, when someone called out from the back of the room, "Stand on a chair, Mrs. Kruger. We can't see you." Others laughed, and, for better or for worse, I was reminded of how odd I must look to them: a short, middle-aged white woman, dressed as if I'd just stepped out of my middle-class home in Boston, although my hair was short and practical and I wore little makeup.

Jackie held my hand to help me climb up onto my chair, and the room grew quiet again as I began to speak. "Dr. King and Malcolm X have created modern-day classics, important books that are being read all over our country. *Othello* is a traditional classic, written by the great playwright William Shakespeare, required reading in many high schools and critical for any student wanting to go to college. The anthology of poems I purchased has some wonderful old poems, as well as modern works by black poets. These are works that our teenagers need to explore."

Dr. Burton took over from there, saying, "I suggest that the PTA wait a week before making any decisions. Each of us should use that time to read the books and understand why Mrs. Kruger believes they are appropriate for her students before we consider banning them." There was a hum of approval throughout the room. A few "Amens" rang out, as if we were in church.

Before any of the board members could respond to Dr. Burton's comments, a young black man stood on his chair and began to speak. "Most of you don't know me. I've come from out of town because I heard about your meeting tonight and was excited that y'all are thinking about bringing books by Martin Luther King and Malcolm X into the school, and I couldn't wait to meet whoever was spearheading the effort. I thought it was going to be some black militant guy wearing an Afro. Man, was I surprised to see this tiny little white lady instead. I can't believe y'all are talking about stopping her from teaching this stuff. You should get down and kiss her feet."

The room was charged with emotion as everyone considered his words. Jackie stood to speak again, but when she tried, her voice broke. When it was clear she couldn't continue, the chairperson adjourned the meeting, promising there would be further discussion when the PTA next met.

Parents assuring me of their support immediately surrounded me. Jackie and I were hugged over and over as people thanked us for daring to speak out. One mother placed her arms protectively around Jackie and said to everyone, "If something is going on at this school that makes a teacher cry, then we parents have a responsibility to look into it. And we will."

ELEVEN

LEAVE *the* BOOKS

To Jo, who was hurt for the cause.

—WRITTEN ON THE FLYLEAF OF *SOUL ON ICE*
BY HER OLDER BROTHER, PHILIP, IN A VOLUME HE
PRESENTED TO HER ON HER TWELFTH BIRTHDAY

February 1969
Jo (11 years old)

I miss Philip. I could talk with him about all kinds of stuff, and he'd understand. Of course I mean boys. Every once in a while he'd get all big-brothery worried, but mostly he'd just listen. I wish I could have told him about the boy I met at the high school dance. Billy is older than me, a ninth grader, and after we danced together, he asked me to go out with him. If Philip had known about it, he would have warned me. But he's up north, living with Connie and Greg.

I was on my own. My mom said it was okay to date Billy because she'd heard from the school librarian that he reads a lot. She thought that because he's kind of awkward and a little bit scrawny and always polite, he'd be safe. He walked me home from school each day and carried my books. That didn't bother me. But then he followed me into the trailer and kissed me. I didn't like that. We were alone and nobody could see us and he kept trying to put his tongue in my mouth. Yeech. At least when I told him to stop, he did, not like the guys at the lake who kept touching me under the water. It lasted only a few days before I told him I didn't want a boyfriend yet, and that was the last I saw of Billy.

I never told Dad about it. He thinks I'm still a baby. He didn't even want to let me go to the school dance. But I'm glad I did. It was fun, and it wasn't even too embarrassing when Mom and Dad got out on the gym floor and everyone stopped dancing to watch them. They actually looked pretty good.

I kind of wish I could dance the way they do. In the movies, it seems like dads always teach their little girls how to dance, but mine never did. I guess he doesn't know that I'd like to learn—

maybe 'cause I'm still a tomboy and would rather shoot baskets with my friends than go out with them. I like to be just one of the guys. I don't want them to treat me any differently because I'm a girl, and they don't.

Later That Week

It was warm for a Saturday afternoon in February. The sky was a clear blue, and there was no breeze. It was hard to believe that just a week ago I was still wearing a jacket. I was kind of bored alone in my bedroom. I tried working on some math problems, but I got stuck, and with Dad out of town, there was nobody to help me. I'd just finished reading *Oliver Twist* and didn't feel like starting a new book. If Philip had been around, maybe we'd have played some music together, but he wasn't.

So I sat staring out the window, not thinking of anything in particular. That's when I saw Thigpen walking across the field behind our trailer, heading for the tree house about a hundred yards away. I thought twice before deciding to follow him. I didn't know him as well as I did some of the other boys, but he always seemed nice enough. I don't think he was any older than the rest of the gang, but he seemed like he was, I guess because he was a little taller and his voice was starting to change. Sometimes I had trouble understanding him and had to ask him to say things twice. I never did figure out whether Thigpen was a nickname, his last name, or his real first name.

Once I decided to go after him, I didn't waste any time. I hollered, "Mom, I'm going out," but didn't wait for an answer. I raced out the back door toward the tree house, trying to catch up with Thigpen before he got there.

Lately, the gang's been spending a lot of time at the tree house. It's in a big old oak tree, kind of like the trees we had in

Newton, only smaller. I think maybe there used to be a lot more of them before folks cleared the fields for cotton. There isn't cotton anymore in the field behind our trailer, but it wasn't that long ago that there was.

Nobody remembers who built the tree house. It isn't much —just a platform without any walls. To get up, you have to climb a half dozen boards that someone nailed into the trunk. The bigger kids can jump down, but I'm scared to try. It's a great hiding place, because once you're up in the tree, nobody can see you, especially if there are leaves. Sometimes I go even if my friends aren't there, because I like to lie down and stare up at the sky and just think about things, or read a book, or even take a nap.

I caught up with Thigpen just as he got to the tree house. He'd already scrambled up the ladder by the time I could say hello. Then he reached down and helped me up the last little bit —not that I needed his help. Leaning against the trunk, he asked, "You seen anybody else today?"

I knew he was talking about Clarence, Toda-Jack, and Flit. "Nope," I answered. "It's been pretty quiet." I was hoping the others might show up. It was kind of awkward sitting there with Thigpen, and I didn't know what to say.

"Maybe that's them now," he said, gesturing across the field at four boys cutting over from the houses along Green Street.

"No, they're too big."

"Yeah."

As they got closer, I recognized George, our neighbor from across the street. But the first one up the ladder was Pitch, one of my friends' big brothers. He's older, a senior in high school, and he's always ignored me. He'd never before come up into the tree house with us. But this time, he seemed kind of friendly and said, "What you doin' playin' up here?"

"Nothin'," Thigpen answered.

"Then we goin' to do nothin' with you," said one of the boys I didn't recognize. Then Pitch sat down next to me and put his arm around my shoulder, pulling me in close to him. At first I thought he was wrestling with me, the way he sometimes did with his little brothers, and I didn't mind that. But then he moved his hand down toward my chest, saying, "What we got here?"

"Stop it," I tried to say, but nothing came out. I couldn't believe what he was doing, and I pushed his hand away. All he did was laugh and put it back. But this time, he used his other hand to hold me so that I couldn't move. His hands were big enough that he could hold both my hands in his. But not very well. I slipped one of them away and flailed out, accidentally hitting him in the face when I tried to push his hand away from my shirt. He pulled me even closer to him and said, "Now, why you doing that? I'm just tryin' to be friendly."

"Cut it out," Thigpen yelled, standing up and trying to shove Pitch away from me, but Pitch just shoved him back, and he fell onto the floor of the tree house. Then he crawled to the makeshift ladder and started to climb down. I didn't want him to leave. Before he reached the ground, Pitch ordered, "George, stop him. Don't let him get away." So George jumped down and held Thigpen by the arm. "Don't you be goin' nowhere. You just set down right here and don' bother us."

In the meantime, Pitch was no longer trying just to put a hand on my chest but had started reaching both his hands up my shirt. Every time he did so, I kept brushing them away, but he kept putting them back. Feeling helpless, I knew my eyes had started tearing up, but I didn't want to cry. Instead, I tried to holler out, but, just like when I'd tried to say "stop" earlier, I couldn't make a sound. Everything was all locked up inside me, as if I was in a nightmare and wanted to holler but had forgotten how.

"Why you fightin' me, girl?" he kept asking. "I ain't gonna hurt you." Then he stopped reaching for my chest and instead tried to put his hands on my pants, between my legs. "I just wanna feel me some of that," he said, reaching around me with one hand and pulling my shoulders against him with the other.

When I pushed his hands away from my crotch, he punched me hard in the leg. I cried out and then started whimpering.

"Take it easy, Pitch," said one of the other boys. "She's just a little girl."

"She's a dirty Jew girl is what she is," he answered. "Listen up, little Jew girl. You stop pushing my hands away, and I won't hit you again."

At first I wouldn't listen to him and kept fighting. And he kept hitting my leg. Finally, I couldn't stand it anymore and let him put his hands on my pants. He kept them there for what seemed like forever. It seemed even worse than the burning pain in my leg, and so I pushed him away. In response, he struck me even harder than before, all the time repeating "dirty Jew" over and over again.

Then one of the boys I didn't know said, "Hey, give me a turn."

"Fair enough," answered Pitch. Then he wrapped his arms around me from behind, pulling me hard against him and totally immobilizing me from the waist up. "She's all yours," he said, as if he were presenting me as a gift.

When the boy moved in close, I started kicking at him. He laughed until I caught him between the legs. I can't have kicked him very hard, because it didn't stop him. It just made him mad, and he punched me in the stomach. I couldn't breathe. I kept gasping, but no air would come in and I started making this weird noise and felt like I was going to throw up.

Pitch let me go, and I sank down to the floor of the tree house and curled up like a baby and hugged myself and rocked back and forth. At some point I must have caught my breath, because all of a sudden, I could talk again. I called out to George, who was still on the ground, making sure that Thigpen didn't leave. I managed to say, "I don't know all these guys, George, but I know you and I can tell everyone what you did." Somehow I thought that might scare him enough to let Thigpen go. It worked even better than that, though, and he said, "Let's get outta here. We gonna be in trouble if anyone finds out about this."

"You right, man," Pitch answered. "She ain't gonna let us do anythin' anyways. Let's go."

With that, they left the tree house and ran off toward town.

I just lay there for a minute, unable to move.

"You okay?" Thigpen called out. When I didn't answer, he climbed halfway up to the tree house. "Can you get down?"

I couldn't answer. I tried a couple of times, but I kept starting to cry, so I bit my lip and shut my eyes tight and just waited for what seemed like forever. Then I heard Thigpen calling my name and saying, "What do you want me to do?"

I picked my head up, opened my eyes, and saw him standing at the top of the ladder. He reached for me but then drew his hand back, like he was afraid to touch me. "Can you get up?"

"I dunno," I answered, still holding back the tears. "Just wait a sec." I tried to breathe deeply, willing myself to stay still. I could hear my father saying, "Crying won't help. It just makes it worse." Finally, I felt ready and sat up. But when I tried to move my legs, the left one felt on fire, right where Pitch had punched me over and over, and I lay down again, trying to figure out what to do.

"Come on," said Thigpen. "I got you." While I'd been resting with my eyes closed, he had climbed up next to me and slipped one arm around my back and under my arm. "Lean on me."

Slowly, he pulled me up until I was standing next to him. My leg was throbbing, but I thought I could manage.

"Should I get some help?"

"No!" I croaked, not wanting anyone to see me like that. Then my leg gave way and I fell against Thigpen. He lowered me back down to the floor of the tree house. After a moment, I crawled to the ladder and tried to get down using just one leg, but I missed a rung and fell a few feet to the ground.

Apparently I hit my head hard when I fell, because the next thing I knew, Thigpen was shaking me awake. He said, "Let me get somebody. I can't carry you home."

"No. I don't want anyone to know about this. You can't say a word."

"How you gonna git home, then?"

"You don't need to carry me. Just let me lean on you."

He helped me stand and put his arm around my back. I tried to hop forward on my good foot, but with every movement, pain shot through me.

"It's no good. I can't do it."

Then Thigpen looked around for a stick. He found a good, sturdy one, over three feet long and thick enough to support me. It even had the beginnings of a branch going off near one end, making it look like a crutch. With Thigpen on one side and my makeshift crutch on the other, I stumbled home. I had to stop so often to rest that it took half an hour to cover the ground that would normally have taken less than five minutes.

As we got to the stairs leading up to the back door of the trailers, Thigpen started to pull away. "I can't stick around," he said. "I don't want yo' momma thinking I did this to you."

Trying hard not to cry, I said, "Just . . . just help me up the stairs."

He did more than that. He sat me down on the top step and

pounded on the door, hollering, "Miz Kruger! Miz Kruger!" Then, as soon as my mother started to open the door, he backed down the stairs and stood there, frozen.

February 1969
Aura (46 years old)

It was the middle of the afternoon. I was in the kitchen, putting the lunch dishes away, when I heard someone pounding at the back door. Assuming that it must be some of the neighborhood kids looking for Jo, I dried my hands and stepped toward the back of the trailer so I could tell them she was already out and about somewhere and they'd just have to go find her if they wanted to play.

As I opened the door, Jo fell in, onto the porch. She'd been sitting up against the door, leaning back on it. When she fell over, she started to wail, her face contorted with pain. After catching her breath, she croaked out, "My leg! My leg!" and curled up in a ball right there on the floor.

I knelt beside her and wrapped my arms around her. She buried her face in my chest, moaning in pain. Not wanting to wait until she could talk again to find out what was wrong, I turned to her friend for an explanation. He looked terrified. It was all he could do to mumble, "We was playing in the tree house, and four boys climbed up and beat on her. I tried to stop them. I did. But I couldn't. I'm sorry." Then he ran away.

I stroked Jo's hair and back, trying to calm her. "Shh, shh," I murmured. "Breathe deeply. Slow down."

After several minutes, she calmed down enough to talk. Between sobs, she said, "It's not just my leg, Mom."

"What do you mean, darling? Tell me what else hurts."

"The boys, they tried to take my clothes off."

"What boys?"

"You know one of them, Mom. He lives right across the street."

"What did they do?"

More sobs. Then, without yet telling me what they'd done, she added, "I said I'd tell on him and he'd get in trouble. He got scared and tried to get the others to stop, but they wouldn't."

"Stop what?"

No answer.

"What did they do?" I asked again, terrified of what I might hear.

"I thought they were going to rape me."

My poor baby. She was only eleven years old and shouldn't even have known what rape was, yet here she was, telling me about her horrifying experience.

This time, I was the one who couldn't speak. *Had* she been raped?

"But they didn't. They didn't."

Wanting to get Jo to her bed, where I could examine her more thoroughly, I helped her up and we stumbled together from the porch into the trailer and then to her bedroom. The whole time she was leaning on me, I kept reminding myself of the many times I'd worked with injured children in Leon's pediatric office in Newton, and I forced myself to remain calm, putting my own emotions on hold so I could help Jo.

Once I had her lying on the bed, I was as gentle as I could be as I started to take off her jeans.

"Stop," she cried. "It hurts too much."

Every movement made her cringe; it took all my strength to continue. Her left leg was terribly swollen above the knee, already black and blue, and I was afraid it was broken. Trying to move it as little as possible, I got her pants back on and she relaxed into her pillow.

I gently rubbed her leg and asked her again to tell me what had happened. "Are you sure they didn't rape you? Do you even know what that is?"

She nodded. "They held me down and kept trying to touch me down there, but I wouldn't let them. So one of the guys kept punching my leg."

I was livid that boys we knew could do this to her—a boy who lived right across the street. I had to talk with him. I told Jo to lie still and that I'd be back in a few minutes. Charles had been hanging about in her doorway, trying to figure out what was going on. I shared with him the gist of the story but not the details, then asked him to sit with his sister while I was gone. For the next twenty-four hours, he barely left her side.

As I walked out front, I saw the boy standing alone in his front yard, staring at our trailer. When he saw me, he looked down, unwilling to face me. I strode across the street, grabbed him by the arm, and dragged him into his house to his grandmother, who was sitting in the front room with the boy's older brother, a young man in his late teens. When I told them what had happened, the grandmother cuffed the younger boy on the ear and said, "I told you not to be messin' with no girls. You got to be stopping dat, or you be in a whole lot of trouble."

I interrupted, saying, "I can't stay to talk. I've got to get Jo to the clinic, and I don't even know how I'm going to get her in the car."

The older brother said, "I'll carry her" and stood up to follow me home without waiting for an answer.

When we got back to Jo's room, she was lying quietly on her bed, half asleep. The young man lifted her in his arms and brought her to my car, gently setting her down in the backseat. She remained limp throughout, seeming to be in a daze. For the first time, I worried she may have sustained head injuries, as well as a broken leg.

I'd called ahead to the clinic, and when we pulled up four nurses were standing outside waiting for us. They slid Jo onto a sheet, and then each one held a corner to carry her inside. The physician in charge while Leon was in Florida was a surgeon named Harvey Sanders. Jo, completely out of it by this time, was taken into an examining room while I told Dr. Sanders everything I knew. He asked me to wait in the corridor while he examined Jo. I did so, but it tore me apart to leave her side.

I sat in a chair I found near the door, twisting this way and that. Finally, unable to contain my impatience any longer, I stood and paced back and forth, waiting to hear the doctor's assessment. As I turned toward the front door of the clinic, I saw the fourteen-year-old from across the street, along with three older boys who I assumed were Jo's attackers. "Mrs. Kruger," one of them began, "we're really sorry. Is she going to be okay?"

I couldn't bring myself to accept their apology. "You should all be arrested," I said, and then walked away. I wasn't about to stand there talking calmly with them while my child lay barely conscious in the room behind us.

A few minutes later, Dr. Sanders found me wandering listlessly. He held me by the shoulders to calm me down and said, "Jo has major contusions on her leg, two broken ribs, and a concussion. It's a miracle that she could walk home, and I don't expect her to be able to put any weight on that leg for several days." He then added that he didn't believe that Jo had been raped.

"I'm going to send her home with you now. You'll need to wake her up every few hours to make sure she hasn't gone into a coma. Can you do that?"

I nodded silently, an icy paralysis stilling my voice.

"She can't walk and she's not ready for crutches. So I'm going to have one of our nurses follow you home and get her to bed."

I stared at him, still voiceless.

"Do you understand what you need to do?" He waited until I nodded again, and then said, "Let's go see her."

I followed him into the examining room, where an aide was helping her into a wheelchair. As I stood with Dr. Sanders, watching her, he said, "I've given her some medication for the pain, and she's doing better."

Better. Although she was conscious, she didn't look better. Her face was pale and tear-stained, her hair a mess, her clothes all dusty. Her eyes, instead of sparkling as they usually did, looked lifeless. I wanted to wrap my arms around her and tell her I wouldn't ever again let anything hurt her, but all I could think about was that it was my fault. I had brought her to this place, where something like this could happen.

I followed wordlessly as the aide wheeled Jo out to my car. He lifted her into it easily, hardly noticing her sixty-five pounds; she looked even smaller as she lay dozing off in the backseat. I drove home in a trance, my body steering while my mind wandered.

A few hours later, another doctor stopped by to check

on Jo. After examining her, she stayed for a couple of hours and we talked. She expressed concern about the lasting psychological effect of the experience and how it might impact Jo's relationships with boys—something that hadn't previously crossed my mind.

After the doctor left, I tried to sleep but couldn't. Every time I closed my eyes, I pictured Jo in the tree house with the boys, and the image tore me apart. I kept blaming myself, thinking it was my fault for having brought her to Mississippi in the first place. And now Leon was thinking about moving us to the inner city of Miami. Could we really do that to our children?

I tossed and turned all night long. It seemed as if every time I fell asleep, the alarm rang and it was time to shake Jo and make sure I could rouse her. When morning arrived, she at least seemed to be feeling better. Dr. Sanders dropped by to see how she was and said we could stop worrying about the concussion. He gave her another shot of pain medication and told me I should let her sleep as long as possible. He added that her ribs and leg would take weeks to heal but the pain would lessen soon.

While we were talking, Leon called from Memphis to say he'd landed and would be home in two hours. I longed to tell him everything, but all I said was, "I can't wait to see you."

After I hung up, Dr. Sanders said, "I'm surprised you didn't tell Leon what happened."

"I couldn't," I answered. "I need him to drive home carefully, with his mind on the road, not our daughter."

Alone again, I puttered about the kitchen, making some chicken-noodle soup for Jo, hoping that one of her favorites might encourage her to eat a little. She hadn't touched the toast I'd given her for breakfast; she'd said that she didn't think she could hold it down. When I brought the soup to her in bed, Charles offered to spoon-feed her, if necessary.

Leaving him to the task he'd set for himself, I returned to my bedroom, hoping to lie down for a bit, the exhaustion starting to overwhelm me. I glanced out the front window as I slipped off my shoes and saw Father Guidry and five nuns coming up the road. I'd never before seen the sisters leave the church and school property and wondered what could possibly have motivated them to be out and about. It dawned on me when they turned into our driveway. They were here to visit us. People at church that morning must have been talking about what had happened to Jo. In fact, the whole town must be talking about it.

I rushed to let them in, grateful for the visit, knowing it would please Jo and help pass the time until Leon got home.

When I opened the door, Sister Rosarita said, "Is Jo well enough for visitors? We'd like to see her."

"Please come in," I said. "She's resting in bed."

As I started to lead the way to Jo's bedroom, Father Guidry whispered that he wished to speak with me alone. So I asked Charles to show the sisters the way, while I remained behind with Father Guidry. He cleared his throat several times before starting to speak. "We have to consider the possibility that those boys weren't acting on their own, that they were set up—possibly even paid—to attack your daughter."

"Why—"

"I know it's difficult to contemplate. But this may have been politically motivated."

I stared at him in disbelief, my head spinning as the implications of his words struggled to take root. "You mean that Leon's work—"

"No, Mrs. Kruger. He's been working at the clinic for almost two years now, and folks have accepted that. I'm talking about those books that you're trying to bring into your classroom."

"What do you mean?" I asked, not really wanting to hear his answer.

"There are some people who want you to leave town. They think that what you're doing in the classroom is dangerous, and they don't want their children exposed to inflammatory ideas."

"But they aren't inflammatory. They—"

"You don't need to explain it to me, Mrs. Kruger. I understand. But not everyone does. They're scared that their children will act in a way that offends the KKK, and that they'll be in danger as a result."

"So you think someone told these boys to beat up my daughter so that I'd stop teaching?"

"I don't have all the answers, and I may be wrong about this. It may have been boys acting like boys and it just got a little out of hand."

How could he say that? Things hadn't just gotten a little out of hand. Jo was still lying in her bed, barely able to move.

As if reading my mind, he added, "I know this is difficult. But whatever reasons the boys had, we have a major problem now."

"What do you mean?"

"If the KKK finds out that four black boys attacked a white girl, they might burn down the whole town in retaliation."

"We'd never say anything. We don't even know anyone in the Klan."

"Everybody in town already knows. Word is bound to get out. I hate to say it, but for the well-being of the town, I think it's time for you to go back to Boston."

"But—"

"I wouldn't say it if I didn't feel strongly about this. We cannot ignore what happened."

"Our leaving won't change anything," I pleaded, not wanting to believe that everything had fallen apart so quickly.

"Unfortunately, it won't. But if you're gone, people will stop talking about it and the KKK will be less likely to get involved. If I'm right, then getting you out of the classroom and away from Mound Bayou is imperative. It's time for you to go."

For a moment, I could hardly breathe. Forcing myself to control the turbulence inside me, I walked quietly into Jo's room, thanked the sisters for coming to the house, and walked them and Father Guidry to the front door.

When I went to check on Jo again, she was awake, talking softly and laughing with Charles. He had just made a joke about Jo's waking up to see all the sisters surrounding her and thinking she'd died and gone to heaven. While I found it too morbid for my taste, Jo enjoyed his humor, and it was the first time I'd seen her laugh since she'd stumbled through the back door. When she tried to sit up a moment later, she found she could do so without too much pain. Seeing this, I asked, "Do you think you could get up and sit in the dining room?"

"Yeah, why?"

"Dad should be home any minute, and I don't want

him to be hit with everything the moment he walks in the door." Since the early days of our marriage, Leon had always wanted a few minutes to relax before he heard about any problems that had come up during the day. Even now, while I was terribly upset about all that had happened, I tried to be the good wife and keep everything as normal as possible.

Accepting my explanation, Jo got out of bed. With Charles on one side and me on the other, we helped her to the dining room table and settled her in one chair, with her legs resting on another. The three of us with the dog and cat at our feet were the image of domestic tranquility.

Moments later, I heard the front door open and Leon came bounding in as he had so many times over the years, his face alight with excitement. It was obvious that he was in high spirits, delighted by his trip and happy to be home. Normally, my own spirits would have lifted to meet his, but not this day.

I hadn't planned on telling him what had happened right away, but he picked up the dog and playfully started to place him on top of Jo's outstretched legs. Charles, Jo, and I all yelled in unison, "Stop!"

Leon froze, the dog barely an inch above Jo's bruised leg. He stared at us in bewilderment, put Pepper on the floor, and then asked what was wrong. I spent the next twenty minutes telling him as he listened quietly. Then he calmly picked up the phone to call Dr. Sanders. They conversed physician to physician, and by the end of their conversation, Leon was optimistic that the physical crisis was over. Only then did his parental instincts take hold. He went to Philip's bedroom, found a baseball bat in the closet, and walked out the front door. He wandered the neighborhood for over an hour, looking for the boys who'd attacked Jo. He told me later it was a good thing he didn't find them, because he didn't know what he would have done had he been successful.

By the time he returned, he was ready to talk. I told him we should leave Mound Bayou in the next couple of days. "Absolutely not," he said. "We'll stay through June, just as we planned. This doesn't change a thing."

"But it does, Leon. Father Guidry said—"

"What does he have to do with anything?"

"Please just let me explain."

Leon began to change his mind when I said it was Father Guidry who had told us to go, that the incident may have been politically motivated, and that we would be placing the town in danger if we stayed. Still not convinced, he went in to talk with Jo, who was once again lying in her bed.

"Do you want to leave?"

"Yes," she mumbled.

"Are you afraid of staying?"

"No."

"What is it, then?"

"I can't go back to school."

"Why not? You'll be a lot better in a few days. We can get you some crutches if you need them."

"That's not it, Daddy."

My heart broke as I stood in the doorway, listening to the two of them. She hadn't called him Daddy since she was a little girl.

Leon must have felt the same way, for he sat on the edge of the bed and started stroking her hair. "What is it, baby?"

She shook her head, silent.

"Is something else bothering you?"

Silence. Another shake of her head.

"Talk to me. Tell me why you can't go back."

"Everybody will know what happened, what those boys did to me, how they . . ."

Then she stopped talking, unable to make herself say it out loud.

I never knew whether it was Father Guidry's pleas for us to leave or Jo's reluctance to return to school, but Leon was finally convinced of the need to leave town. He didn't even wait until Monday morning to call the University of Miami to ask if he could start his new job in a couple of weeks, instead of at the beginning of July. He called the man who would be his new boss and told him what had happened. The answer: "Come as soon as you can. The sooner, the better."

Having settled that, he next asked, "How soon can we leave?" Jo was getting better by the hour, and Leon assured me she was well enough to travel. She still spent most of her time in bed and asleep but was clearly gaining strength. As soon as we tied up a few loose ends at work and packed clothes for the trip and the first few weeks in Miami, we could go. We decided we could accomplish everything by Monday afternoon and begin our trip the morning after.

Over breakfast, we discussed the logistics for the day, beginning with whether Charles should go to school. He wanted to stay home with Jo, and we were nervous about his being out and about, concerned that if the incident two days earlier was politically motivated, he might be in danger. Also, we didn't want to leave the children at home without an adult. So we agreed that I would go to school briefly and pick up my personal belongings, and once I got home, Leon could go to the clinic.

When I walked into my classroom, a substitute was lecturing about *Of Mice and Men*, which my students were supposed to have finished reading over the weekend. I felt a twinge of jealousy. This was my class. They shouldn't be listening to a lecture; if I'd been teaching, we would have pulled our chairs into a circle and discussed the book together. I'd be trying to get them to search for its relevance in their own lives.

As soon as they saw me, the students started to ask questions, but I held my finger to my lips and shook my head, indicating that they should continue listening while I packed up my desk. They did as I asked, but I could feel them watching me as I opened the top desk drawer and began to put my personal belongings in a paper bag. Staring into the drawer, I hardly noticed the papers and pens there; instead I saw colors swirling about as I thought of my students. I longed to hug each of them, to assure them that they'd done nothing wrong, that my leaving had nothing to do with them. Instead, I reached blindly into the drawer, grasping at the few supplies remaining.

Next, I went to the four boxes of books sitting undisturbed on the floor. As I stared at the books, I thought about how much trouble they'd caused and wondered once again if the attack on Jo was a result of my attempts to introduce black literature into the class-room. When I picked up one of the boxes to take it to my car, one student called out, "Leave the books, Mrs. Kruger."

"We'll read them," said another.

Several started chanting, "Leave the books. Leave the books." And then the whole class joined in.

I put down the box and looked at them silently, waiting for them to be quiet. Gradually the chanting stopped, and then Johnny said, "We promise that we'll read them."

Encouraged by this sign that I had made a difference for my students, I left the books, blew them a kiss, walked slowly out of the building with the rest of my belongings, and drove home.

As soon as I arrived, Leon took off for the clinic, promising to be back in time for dinner. I looked in on Charles and found him in his room, packing his things. I sat on the edge of his bed. I wanted to ask how he felt about leaving Mound Bayou, whether he minded being uprooted again.

As if reading my mind, he said, "Mom, I'm going to miss Mound Bayou, but I'm glad we're going to Florida. I think I'll like it there."

"Why is that, Charles?" I asked, patting the edge of the bed. He so rarely talked about anything other than his books and music that I welcomed the opportunity to get him to open up a little.

"Grandma and Grandpa will be there. And the beach. It'll be like being back on Cape Cod."

Of the whole family, he was the one who missed our old life the most, especially those long, lazy summers at the beach.

"Yes, I think it will."

"I'll miss Sister Rosarita."

"She's been a good teacher."

"She has."

"What about your friends here?"

His silent gaze reminded me that we had taken him away from the few friends he'd had in Newton and made it painfully clear that he'd never really made new ones in Mound Bayou. Florida would be good for him. My folks would make him feel loved, and the schools would be better. He'd have classmates who could interact with him on a level he hadn't known since his arrival at St. Gabriel's.

"You'll make friends in Miami," I said, putting my hand on his cheek. I wanted to hug him tightly, to tell him everything would be all right. But at twelve years old, he knew better. Nor did he especially want my hugs.

Leaving his room, I walked aimlessly about the trailers for a few minutes, finding it hard to believe we'd be leaving the following morning. Then I sat with Jo, watching her sleep.

I was just about to start sorting through what to take with us to Miami when the phone rang. It was Mr. Moore, the principal of the high school. "I know it's a bad time for you, Mrs. Kruger, but can you come talk to the students? They're roaming the halls and refusing to sit in class. They're mad because they think the school board fired you for bringing in those books. I've tried to tell them that's not true, but they won't believe me. They want to hear it from you."

I said I'd be happy to come but didn't feel safe leaving the children alone. Since Leon would be at work for the rest of the day, I had to stay home. He said he'd call back in a few minutes. When he did, he said he'd arranged for a friend to stay with Charles and Jo and that I should go straight to the gym as soon as she arrived.

I got into my car and drove one last time to the school. It was only February, but the weather had already turned warm. I could feel the humidity pressing in on me as I wondered what I would say to the students. Then it occurred to me: all I had to do was tell them the truth. They deserved that.

The cool air inside the school felt good, refreshing. I stopped in the doorway of the gym and looked in. Every student in the school was sitting quietly in the stands, and all the teachers were lined up along the cinder-block walls. Mr. Moore was speaking into a microphone, leaning in a little too closely, so it was making that awful feedback. He was telling the students that he'd sent for me and I would be arriving shortly.

One of the students noticed me standing there and called out quietly, "There she is." Mr. Moore stopped midsentence. Then one student began to applaud. A moment later, the entire room was clapping, and the tears began streaming down my face despite my best efforts to stop them.

At first Mr. Moore tried to settle the students by holding out his hands, palms down. Then, with a tight smile, he stepped back from the mic and began clapping as well. I nodded to him and mouthed "Thank you" as I made my way to an empty chair in the first row. Before sitting down, I stood and looked at the students and held my finger to my lips in a gesture they'd seen me use many times before when I wanted them to be quiet. Almost immediately, the clapping stopped and Mr. Moore began to speak.

"Thank you for coming, Mrs. Kruger," he said, looking directly at me. "As you can see, the students are eager to hear from you. A rumor has spread that you are leaving

Mound Bayou because you have been fired. People say that this is a result of you bringing black literature into the classroom. Before I ask you to stand and tell everyone that this isn't true, I want to tell you that I appreciate what you've done for this town. Every Negro student here—no, every black student—has benefited from your efforts." It was the first time I'd heard him use the term "black" instead of "Negro."

When I got up to speak, I said, "You probably remember that I started each of our speech classes by asking you to make impromptu speeches. I didn't know at the time that I would be making one on this, my last day with you. But here I am. My daughter Jo was beaten up over the weekend. I know that some people are saying that she was raped. She wasn't. But she was severely hurt. She has two broken ribs, a concussion, and contusions on her leg that are so bad she can't walk. It will be many weeks before she is well again."

I told them of the advice we'd received from Father Guidry, whom they all knew and respected. I said he'd asked us to leave Mound Bayou as quickly as possible for the safety of the town. I told my students how much I hated to leave them, that I treasured the time we'd spent together in the classroom, and that I wouldn't endanger them by staying.

I concluded by saying, "I love you. And I will miss you."

As I turned to leave, a number of them called out, "What about the books?"

I turned back and said what I thought might ease the tense situation. "All adults want what's best for you, parents and teachers alike. We have many different ideas about education and do not always agree about what the right thing to do is. You know my beliefs. You have the books. Read them."

Then the students came running out of the stands and surrounded me, blocking my way. Tyree hugged me tightly. Frag promised that he'd read the books. Linda's eyes teared up as she held my hand. It took a long time for me to make my way to the door, and as I walked out of the building, I felt my throat tighten as I thought of how much each student meant to me.

As soon as I arrived home, I checked in on the children and then lay down on the living room couch, desperately in need of a break. Within moments, however, Leon walked in, looking somewhat sheepish.

"I need to ask you to do something, Aura," he said.

"You make it sound like it's something I won't want to do."

"You probably won't. The mother of one of the boys visited me at the clinic and asked if they could speak with you."

"One of the boys? You mean—"

"Yes."

"I can't," I said, holding my hand over my mouth and shaking my head. "You can't ask me to do this."

"They're here."

"Now?"

"I left them on the porch. Please—it's important."

I looked past him out the sliding glass door and saw a woman standing there with one of the boys I'd seen in the hospital. He looked smaller now, almost frail, staring down at his feet. His mother was speaking to him, a stern expression on her face, and he was nodding slowly. Part of me, a very small part, felt sorry for him. "I'll talk with them," I said. "But don't expect me to forgive him."

Leon went out to the porch and brought them in, gesturing for the mother to sit on the chair next to the couch. The boy remained standing, his head still bent.

There was an awkward silence, as if everyone were waiting for me to get things started. I didn't. Finally, the boy's mother spoke. "Thank you, Mrs. Kruger, for letting us in. My boy, Johnnie, he has something to say to you."

When he didn't speak up, all I could say was, "Well?" in an icy manner.

"Go ahead, Johnnie," said Leon. "Say what you want to say."

The boy mumbled something I couldn't understand.

"You better speak mo' clearly, boy, so they can hear you."

"I'm sorry."

"That's all?" I said, finding it impossible to be generous.

"We didn't mean to hurt her. We was just havin' some fun."

Fun? How could he describe what they did to my little girl as fun? And why did Leon want me to listen to this? Did he really want me to forgive this boy? Or did he think I might feel better for putting a more human face on Jo's attackers?

Then Johnnie said something that jerked me back to the moment. I wasn't quite sure I'd heard him right. "How long did you say you were up in the tree house?"

"About forty-five minutes."

Forty-five minutes? Forty-five minutes! I'd had no idea that Jo's ordeal had lasted that long. The boy's mother reached over and put a hand on my shoulder, trying to comfort me, but I turned away. Leon ushered mother and son out as I buried my face in a cushion. I don't know how long I sat there crying, but eventually I felt someone's arms around me. I turned and recognized one of the nurses who had been working at the local hospital long before the Boston contingent arrived. She stayed with me until I regained my composure and then took me back to the other trailer, where Leon was preparing dinner.

After we finished eating, Jo fell asleep and Charles went to his room to finish packing. Leon and I stood in the kitchen, cleaning up in silence, unable to talk about the revelation regarding how long and severe the attack had been. Just as we put away the last of the dishes, we heard a knock at the front door. About twenty of my students stood outside, asking if they could come in to say good-bye. Leon invited them into the living room, where they settled on the chairs, the sofa, the piano bench, and the floor. We talked for a while, reminiscing about favorite times in my class.

"Remember that day when Rivers busted into the room and was gonna throw a brick at us?"

"Was you scared, Miz Kruger?"

"Yes."

"You were? Didn't seem like it. You just told him to put it down, that it was your doorstop."

"I was scared that one of you was going to get hurt. I had to stop him."

"You was always lookin' out for us."

"How about the time you took us to Memphis to see that movie?"

"And we got to sit where the white folks do."

"Miz Kruger, you really think there'll be a time when nobody'll think twice about lettin' us do stuff like that?"

"I do, Thelma, I really do. And you are the ones who are going to make that happen."

When they'd been there for about half an hour,

Nathan, a shy, quiet boy sitting on the floor, said, "Is Jo well enough to come in? I have something I want to give her."

Leon, who had been shuttling back and forth from the kitchen, bringing whatever snacks he could find, said, "I'll go see."

A moment later, he returned with her by his side. He had one arm about her, holding her up so that she didn't need to put any weight on her left foot. As they came through the door, the students on the floor all scooted away from the center of the room to make space for them. Leon helped Jo to the newly vacated space and lowered her gently to the floor. One of the students grabbed a pillow from the couch and placed it under her head. Another covered her with his jacket so she wouldn't be cold.

Then Nathan knelt beside her and presented her with a vase he'd been cradling in his hands. "I made this last week in art class, and I want you to have it. Whenever you look at it, I want y'all to think of all the folks in Mound Bayou who care about you and are sorry 'bout what happened. Don't just remember what happened a couple of days ago. Think about all the good times you've had. And we all want you to know we 'preciate what you and your family been doin' for us." With that, he hugged Jo gently and placed the vase next to her. It wasn't long before she was sound asleep, her hands clasped tightly around the gift.

A few minutes later, one of the students pointed out that there were others waiting outside, milling about in our front yard. The first group left through the back door at the same time that another came in through the front. Over the next few hours, it seemed as if a hundred students streamed through, each staying for ten to fifteen minutes. One after another, the students said how sorry they were to see us go, how much we were appreciated, and how they would never forget us. The last of the students left just after midnight. It had been a bittersweet evening, one we would remember vividly for the rest of our lives.

In the morning, Leon scrambled about the kitchen, making breakfast from the little bit of food left over from the night before. We planned to get an early start, but the arrival of another group of visitors delayed our departure. In the same way my students had come the night before, Leon's colleagues from the clinic came all morning. Many said they'd tried to visit the previous evening, but when they'd driven by and seen all the students waiting their turn to come in, they'd decided to leave the night to the teenagers and come in the morning instead.

It was almost noon when the last of Leon's colleagues left. Only then were we able to pack the car and get Jo settled comfortably in the backseat. As Leon held the door open for me, he squeezed my hand one last time to assure me all would be well. As we pulled out onto the road, I found it hard to believe that never again would I view Mound Bayou as our home. And I knew that our time in Mound Bayou had changed me forever.

TWELVE

BACK *to* MOUND BAYOU

When time passes, it's the people who knew you whom you want to see; they're the ones you can talk to. When enough time passes, what's it matter what they did to you?

—JOHN IRVING, *THE CIDER HOUSE RULES*, 1985

August 2008
Jo (51 years old)

The Illinois Central railroad tracks are gone, the line shut down since my parents brought my two brothers and me to live in Mound Bayou forty years ago. Nobody in town gets awakened in the middle of the night by the rumbling of a train speeding through, and mothers no longer warn their children about racing across the unguarded tracks. Although much of the younger generation has fled north to find jobs, the town population is close to double what it was in 1967. There are more houses now, and they all have electricity and indoor plumbing. Instead of dirt and mud, the roads are paved.

Old Highway 61 is still the main street of town, but there are fewer stores on it and the hustle and bustle of small-town life in the middle of the twentieth century is gone. Now there's a four-lane freeway a mile farther west—the new Highway 61— that knocks half an hour off the hundred-mile drive south from the Tennessee border. Most people travel on that new road and never even know the town is there.

Clarence Holmes, my best friend back when I lived there, told me to take this new highway when I came. I'd called him in July to let him know I'd be visiting for a few days. "You'll stay with Lucille and me," he said.

It wasn't a question. It had been over forty years since I'd seen Clarence, yet the connection was still strong. If I was going to be in town, I would be their guest.

"I appreciate it, Clarence. But it's not just me. I'll be traveling with my daughter, Elizabeth. Is that okay?"

"No problem. Is she your oldest?"

"Yeah. She's almost twenty-four, and she'll be taking pictures and writing notes."

"What for?"

"I'm working on a book about when my family lived there. That's what I wanted to talk with you about. Can you set up some interviews for me?"

"Sure. Who do you want to talk with?"

"Mostly my mom's old students. Maybe some of the teachers."

"I can do that."

"And any of my dad's colleagues who are still around. Your folks, of course."

"Of course. Anyone else?"

"The four guys who beat me up."

He didn't answer.

"You still there?"

"You really want to talk to them? Are you sure?"

"I am."

"Look, I'll try. But I don't know if any of them will want to get together. You know this is kind of weird, don't you?"

"I know. It's what I want."

"Okay."

Then we started talking about logistics. Although he was now the father of two and I was returning as a fifty-one-year-old mother of four, the years faded away as we planned my trip. I told him that Elizabeth and I would meet up at the Memphis airport; I'd be flying in from Texas and she from Philadelphia. I'd rent a car and we'd drive down Highway 61, repeating the trip I took when I was ten years old.

"The old highway's gone," he said. "You'll have to take the new one."

I could practically taste my disappointment. I'd really been looking forward to experiencing one more time the beautiful desolation of that drive I remembered so well.

"Okay, but it looks like the old road is still there in spots. I can catch it coming in from Shelby, right?"

"Yeah, but don't do that. The new highway will take you right to the clinic. We can meet up there. You know I work there, right?"

I didn't know that. I knew very little about Clarence or the rest of his family, as my early letters had gone unanswered. "What do you do?"

"I'm a physical therapist. You just come in to the front desk and ask for me, and I'll show you around town."

Then I realized why he wanted me to take the new highway. It wasn't just that it was faster. He didn't want my trip down Memory Lane to start without him. He wanted to be my guide, and I was perfectly content to let him play that role.

✒

HEADING SOUTH FROM MEMPHIS to Mound Bayou on a warm summer morning, my twenty-three-year-old daughter, Elizabeth, behind the wheel, I let my mind wander back to the day I met Clarence. It was my first week in the fifth grade at St. Gabriel's mission school, and I had time to kill until my father finished work and could drive my brothers and me to the motel in Cleveland where we were staying until the trailers that were to be our home for the next two years arrived. Philip and Charles had chosen to wait inside the school, but I walked to the basketball court out back, looking for a pickup game. Nobody was there and I didn't have a ball, so I kept walking. Beyond the court was a big, overgrown field with grass so high that it was difficult to find a path through it, and I quickly gave up. Returning to the street, I strolled toward the railroad tracks, passing a couple of houses before I noticed several boys around my age playing football in the vacant lot that would soon be our front yard.

"Can I play?" I asked.

They were astonished. Not only was I a girl, I was a white girl. Not knowing what else to do, they said okay. They even gave me the ball on the first play, and before I knew it, several boys had tackled me.

From that day on, Clarence and I spent countless hours together, roaming the neighborhood, playing in each other's homes, tossing a football around, and shooting hoops. He was willing to treat me like one of the guys and made sure the other boys did as well. But when I told him my name was Jo, he said, "That's a boy's name. I'm calling you Joey." And that's how I was known in Mound Bayou from then on.

Elizabeth pulled me back to the present when she said, "We're crossing the border, Momma. We're leaving Tennessee."

I'd told her to watch for the billboard that said WELCOME TO MISSISSIPPI, THE MAGNOLIA STATE and had a picture of a Civil War–era plantation house, but it was nowhere in sight. Instead there was a sign with the words WELCOME TO MISSISSIPPI. IT'S LIKE COMING HOME, accompanied by a drawing of a magnolia flower.

"Pull over so I can take a look," I said. "I can't believe that sign is gone. I thought it would be there forever."

"I guess it makes sense. It doesn't sound like it was very politically correct."

"It wasn't."

Elizabeth knew all about the sign and how it in some way represented our family's journey from the Northeast to Mound Bayou. All her life she'd heard her grandmother and me talk about this little town where I'd spent two years of my childhood, and she was more than willing to take time off from her job as a consultant to join me for my trip back in time.

I knew that a lot would have changed, but I wasn't quite ready for how the new Highway 61 was so different from the old one I'd known as a child. Now there were four lanes of fresh pavement. Instead of endless fields of cotton on either side of it, there was an endless stream of billboards; instead of shotgun shacks, a string of middle-class housing developments, bedroom communities for Memphis commuters.

Twenty miles into Mississippi, we stopped at a state visitors' center, where I asked the lady behind the counter if it was still possible to drive on Old Highway 61. "Why on earth would you want to go there?" she asked, her thick Southern drawl only partially masking her disdain for the tiny black communities that were all that was left along the old route.

When I told her I used to live in that area as a child, her attitude warmed. No longer was I some Northerner invading her state—I was part of the family. "What town? Maybe I know your family."

"Mound Bayou, about eighty miles south of here."

She shook her head. "I'm afraid I don't know it."

Then she told us to take a small road heading west toward the Mississippi River and we'd find the old highway. In a matter of minutes, we'd turned south onto it and it was exactly as I had pictured—barely wide enough for one lane in each direction, the pavement crumbling into the dirt at the edges, the cotton fields starting right after the dirt and stretching to the horizon.

My mother had often described her initial reaction to those endless fields, saying how desolate they were and how depressing she had found them upon her first trip to Mississippi. But I loved them. They were part of my childhood.

Instead of seeing the poverty of the area, I saw myself at ten years old, ready for whatever adventure life tossed my way.

Some things were different. A few of the towns we passed now had traffic lights, where before there weren't even stop signs. The houses looked more prosperous, sturdy structures having replaced most of the old shacks. The few that still stood looked much as I remembered, with their peeling paint, their rusted sheet-metal roofs, and their boarded-up windows. Yet many of them now sported window air-conditioning units and satellite dishes. Forty years earlier, folks had been too poor to afford such luxuries; they had sat on their front porches in Mound Bayou to cool off in the evenings, sleep delayed until the stifling heat of the long summer days had a chance to disappear into the night.

❧

ALTHOUGH THE CLINIC WAS the same one my father had opened in 1967, it looked completely different. The Delta Health Center (the word "Tufts" dropped from the name when funding was picked up through SUNY-Stonybrook) was now a modern brick edifice surrounded by crepe myrtle trees in full bloom, their pink blossoms lending a picturesque feel to the building. When I was a child, it stood alone in an empty field, constructed from several prefabricated units stuck together.

It made me proud of my dad to see how the clinic he'd started had grown into something so permanent. I smiled at the memory of the Saturday morning when our pancake breakfast was interrupted by a loud rumble outside. Running to the front window to investigate, we saw trucks rolling down the street, towing the modules. Dad flew out the door, wearing nothing but his khaki shorts, and shouted, "That's my clinic! There go my buildings!" Then he ran down the street, chasing the trucks. He must have gone a hundred yards before he raced back to the house to don his shirt and shoes.

Elizabeth laughed when I told her the story. "I can just imagine Grandpa Leon running down the middle of the street," she said as she parked the car. My own laughter died away as I looked about the lot, populated by a selection of very old cars that made it obvious that many of the patients were still quite poor. Once we were inside, that realization grew stronger. In the restroom, most of the doors on the stalls had fallen off, and the few that remained hung at precarious angles, their hinges rusty and loose. It looked like the place hadn't been painted in years, and water stains marked the ceiling. Patients slumped in their chairs, biding their time until they were called in for their appointments. All were black. Most looked poor, their sun-dresses and blue jeans worn thin. No longer did patients dress up in their Sunday best to visit the doctor. And despite the presence of several young children, there were no toys or books to help them while away the time. An antiseptic scent permeated the room.

Elizabeth, checking out a community bulletin board, was struck by the prominent announcements about classes where adults could earn their high school degree. This was clearly an area where much of the population hadn't finished high school. We hadn't really known what to expect, so I can't say that we were surprised. In some ways, we had to consider it progress. After all, back in the 1960s a lot of students dropped out before graduation and nobody thought twice about it. At least now an effort was being made to reach out and help.

Pulling away from the bulletin board, we found our way to the physical therapy section, where Clarence had told us we'd find him, but he was out. And he hadn't left word for us about when he'd be back. I worried that he'd changed his mind about hosting us, that we weren't really welcome in town. I'd been afraid of that ever since my editor, Alexandra Shelley, had advised me to visit, saying, "If you want to write an honest, authentic book about your family's time in Mississippi, you have to go."

I'd cringed at the thought. As an eleven-year-old, I couldn't begin to think about returning to school and facing all my friends after I'd been molested. As a fifty-one-year-old, I was still wary, so I resisted. At first I was convinced that the reason for my reluctance was clear, that it was tied to the events of our last few days in town. Eventually, however, I had to admit to myself that it wasn't. I'd long since dealt with the aftermath of having been beaten up. There was something else. Something that took me a while to figure out.

Unlike my brother Charles, I had not considered my mother's rosy portrayal of our time in Mound Bayou to be "the big lie." I'd believed her when she'd promised that it would be the adventure of a lifetime, that we would be welcomed and appreciated, and that one day we would write about it and become famous.

I didn't want to spoil the image I'd clung to all these years. I didn't want to face the possibility that my brother might be right, that perhaps we had been not accepted but merely tolerated, that we were interlopers, perhaps helping the community in some ways but hurting it in others. And I didn't want to return to Mound Bayou only to learn that my mother hadn't been a fantastic teacher from her first moment in the classroom.

I didn't tell Alexandra what I figured out. I pretended instead to have overcome my reluctance to deal with the memory of my ordeal, not yet ready to say out loud that I had doubts about what I would find were I to return. Then, like my mother before me, I put my doubts aside and made plans for a visit. And I'm glad I did. Forty-one years was a long time to wait to resolve the doubts I hadn't even acknowledged I had.

Fortunately, those doubts disappeared after Clarence pulled up in his minivan, jumped out without bothering to park, and engulfed me in a huge bear hug. If I hadn't been watching for him, I never would have recognized him. He wore hospital scrubs and towered over me, a former high school football player who looked the part. The smile was the same, though, kind of big and goofy.

As I listened to him say, "Joey. Little Joey Kruger," the years fell away. My eyes watered as I let the memories wash over me: Clarence and I the same height, standing together as we watched the truckers back my family's two trailers into the lot where we'd first played football, two ten-year-old children gawking at the speed and skill with which the trailers were un-hitched and set on the cement-block foundation that had been built prior to their arrival. Clarence's parents coming to our new home to play bridge with my parents, their conversation flowing just as it had when my parents had gotten together with their best friends in Newton. Clarence laughing when a friend's horse tossed me into the drainage ditch that ran along Township Road.

Forty-one years earlier, I'd moved to Mound Bayou a naive ten-year-old girl, believing that I could handle anything that came my way. Returning as an adult, I realized that the strength I'd developed during our time there gave me the ability to do just that. I was more than ready for Clarence to accompany me on my visit to the past.

⁓

DRIVING EAST ON TOWNSHIP ROAD—now called McGinnis Street—we arrived at the Catholic church, a tiny red brick building, much smaller than I remembered from the weekly services we attended when I was in the fifth grade at the mission school. The double wooden doors opened directly into the main room of the church, its perfect symmetry destroyed by a recent add-on reflecting a still-active congregation. Standing there, looking about the chapel, I could hear Father Guidry addressing all the students on our first day of school, telling us how fortunate we were to have families who cared enough about us to allow us to obtain a good education. I would have loved to see him, to get answers to questions about my past and all that happened in Mound Bayou, but he had long since passed away, and Sister Rosarita, the school principal, had moved to the East Coast to live in a nursing home for retired nuns.

A few steps beyond the church stood the five-room structure that used to house St. Gabriel's School, where my brothers and I started our education in Mound Bayou. Father Guidry called it a mission school because hardly anybody paid tuition, and those who did paid only three dollars a month.

It had been ten years since the building had functioned as a school. As the town aged, the need for a second elementary school had vanished and the facility had become the St. Gabriel Mercy Center, offering a wide variety of support services. There was a thrift shop where the school cafeteria used to be, a program designed to show parents how to teach their babies and toddlers so they'd be ready for school, a senior day-care program, a library, and a computer learning center. Half of the old auditorium was converted to a sewing-instruction class where women could learn a marketable skill, and the other half was an after-school care program. Finally, there was a GED preparation class where adults who had never completed high school could earn a diploma.

Beverly Johnson, the facility's social worker—who just

happened to be Clarence's cousin—showed us around the center. Learning that fact reminded me of what life in a small town, where everybody knows everybody else, is like. And Clarence seemed to epitomize that fact. Everywhere we went, folks stopped him to stay hello.

The first time it happened was as we were leaving St. Gabriel's. An elderly woman pulled up in a car and started to walk toward the church door. When she saw Clarence, she stopped and said, "My goodness, Clarence, what are you doing here?"

"I'm touring the town with an old friend. Do you remember—"

Before he could finish the thought, she exclaimed, "I know you. You lived here a long time ago. You taught at the high school."

That's when I realized she thought I was my mother. People always told me that we looked alike, but at that moment, I knew for the first time how true it was.

No, ma'am," said Clarence. "You're remembering her momma, Mrs. Kruger. This here is Little Joey."

"That's right. I remember you. You were always up in the trees."

Elizabeth laughed at the thought of her fifty-one-year-old mother climbing trees.

"And you used to wipe tables at Crowe's Bar-B-Q. I heard you did that for pinball money."

Her memory was perfect. I'd spent many afternoons at that restaurant, clearing tables off. Mr. Crowe had paid me by giving me quarters for the pinball machine.

As we got in the car, Clarence turned to Elizabeth and said, "Can you imagine your mother when she was ten years old? The first time I met her, I was playing football after school and she walked right up and said she wanted to play too. We couldn't believe it. We'd heard there were a couple of white families moving to town and that they might have kids our age, but we never thought there'd be a girl who played football."

"I was just thinking about that while we were driving down here," I said, glad that Clarence remembered.

"That first day, we huddled up and decided to give her the ball and then tackle her so hard that she wouldn't want to stay," Clarence added, turning back to Elizabeth.

"I remember," I said.

"You were so funny. Your face was all red from being under that pile, but you just jumped up and ran back to the huddle. So we let you play."

By allowing me into his group of friends, Clarence made my transition into life in Mound Bayou much easier. He came from one of the "elite" families, meaning that they had been there since the town's founding—in 1887, by former slaves—and they'd had property there for generations. His grandfather owned and operated the local cotton gin. His father was the postmaster and his mother was a teacher and nutritionist, both of them college educated. Their home, although small compared with the one my family had in Newton, was much nicer than many of the other houses around, with indoor plumbing and electricity. During my two years in town, I spent many happy hours as a guest there.

⚘

CONTINUING TOWARD TOWN ON Township Road, I noticed that much nicer homes had replaced most of the old shacks. Clarence never used the word "shack" to describe the structures that populated Mound Bayou back in the 1960s. He referred to them as the "old houses" and was pleased that very few still existed, especially within the city limits. He told me how our old neighbor Earl Lucas had been mayor for a while and had obtained quite a bit of federal money to build new houses, thus accommodating the town's growth from the 1,300 residents when we were there to the 2,400 people who lived there now.

Others had focused on bringing new industry to the area, to make up for the jobs lost due to the mechanization of cotton picking and also to allow growth. The clinic was now the area's biggest employer, and many community members had attended college and been trained in the medical profession. Then there was rice farming, which was introduced in the 1990s and successfully brought money into the area, but also mosquitoes.

As we drove around, more changes jumped out at me. All the streets were paved, and there were a lot more of them. There was a new, two-story, redbrick city hall with a police and fire station. Back when we lived in Mound Bayou, there was one police officer and no fire department, and although there was a mayor, I don't think he had an office.

Clarence said that the biggest change was the prevalence of drugs. When we lived there, alcohol was a problem; even very young teenagers got drunk frequently. But—as far as we knew—there were no drugs. Not true anymore. Drugs are to blame for the deaths of several people who were my friends back in elementary school, through either overdoses or drug-related violence.

After cruising around for a few minutes, Clarence pulled up in front of the school, John F. Kennedy Memorial High School, built in 1965, just a couple of years before our arrival. A freshly painted sign stood in front of the school, boasting the school name, the school colors—blue and yellow—and hornet mascot, and the phrase WHERE EVERYBODY IS SOMEBODY. When we stepped into the office, Clarence introduced the principal, Wanda Stringer, a black woman in her late fifties who spoke with authority and a strong sense of pride.

A few minutes into the conversation, the principal told me that her maiden name was Campbell and it was her family that had purchased our trailers when we left town. Life in a small town . . .

Our visit to the high school was cut short when Clarence got a call from his wife, Lucille, saying she was ready for lunch and we should pick her up at her high school in Cleveland, eight miles away. As we drove south along Mound Bayou's main street, I saw how different it was from the bustling place I remembered as a child. Back in the 1960s, the town boasted several bars, a restaurant, a pool hall, a post office, a small grocery store, a Laundromat, several churches, and a little stand where for a nickel we could buy a snow cone. The post office was still there, and a gas station now stood at the intersection of Township Road and Highway 61, but those were the only places showing signs of life. Buildings were boarded up, and the street was relatively empty. Clarence explained that when the new highway came through a little west of town, folks stopped shopping in Mound Bayou and the handful of businesses couldn't survive.

Meeting Lucille, a high school guidance counselor, was a treat. She was one of the friendliest people I'd ever met—not surprising when I considered how outgoing Clarence is. She grew up in a small town in the hills of southern Mississippi and attended a nearby college. She and Clarence met when he was getting his training in physical therapy, and they'd been together for almost thirty years. I don't think I ever saw her when she wasn't smiling, and she frequently spoke about her students as if they were her own children.

Once introductions were finished, accompanied by warm hugs all around, Clarence drove us to a restaurant called

Fermier's. As we walked in, I quickly realized that Elizabeth and I were the only white people there. Later, she told me that while she was going through the buffet line, she heard several comments from some of the younger black men regarding her appearance: "I'd like to hit that." "Hey, baby, what you doin' here?" It reminded me how I used to get comments like that all the time when we lived in Mound Bayou. I hated how awkward it made me feel, how I never knew how to react. But Elizabeth seemed not to mind. She just took it in, along with everything else.

Shortly after we sat down, Clarence pointed out a man named James Farmer, saying that he was the owner of the restaurant. "When James opened up this place, he didn't want to call it Farmer's, because he thought that wasn't classy enough. So he tried to make it sound French by using Fermier's instead."

Obviously yet another good friend of Clarence's, James joined us at our table. After introductions, which included only our names and the fact that I'd lived in Mound Bayou as a child, James said, "What were you doing in Mound Bayou?"

I answered, "My dad was setting up a clinic, and my mom taught at the high school."

"Wait. What's your last name, again? I mean, when you lived here?"

"Kruger."

"Mrs. Kruger? Your mother was Mrs. Kruger? She was my teacher!"

I was impressed that forty years later, he remembered her name without any prompting. As we talked more, it was obvious that he remembered her well because she had made quite an impression on him. In describing her, he said, "She really cared about us and wanted us to do well. She was always telling us to read and said we could do anything we wanted to do, be anything we wanted to be. And she really believed that." He'd taken her words to heart. Although he grew up in one of the poorer families out in the fields near Mound Bayou, he is now the owner of three dry-cleaning stores, a restaurant, and a sports bar.

At this point, Clarence said, "You've got to call your mom and tell her about James."

I did. She knew exactly who he was: "On Founder's Day, my students were decorating a float with flowers made from tissue paper. After they had a huge pile of flowers, we all went outside so they could glue them to the school float. But just as the truck pulling the float started out of the parking lot, it died. James disappeared, and the next thing I knew he was driving back in with another truck, honking his horn and waving out the window."

James couldn't believe that my mother remembered that story. When I relayed the information to him, he grinned like a little kid and said, "That's right. That's exactly what happened. It was my uncle's truck."

After the excitement of the phone call, I asked James about the fact that there were no other white people in the restaurant. He explained that, with the exception of Thursday nights, no white people ever came. Thursday, however, was party night at Delta State University, and the white students loved the food and the price at his restaurant and the fact that the sports bar was right next door, so they would come on Thursday night. James referred to it as both College Night and White Night.

When I asked if there was ever trouble between the white and black customers, he said that the white boys preferred fighting with their fists and knives, but the black boys used guns. He'd had shootings in the parking lot and had to throw out students who started fighting in the restaurant. But he seemed to take it all in stride, as if that were the most natural thing on

Earth, and explained it away by saying the place never had any trouble except on Thursday nights.

After lunch, we dropped off Lucille at her school and headed back to Mound Bayou. Moments after we passed the sign announcing the town's unique history, Clarence pulled off into a service station. At first, I assumed he was just getting gas. I quickly realized, however, that the older gentleman who had come over to talk with Clarence wasn't just saying hello. He kept staring at me, as if trying to recognize me. It was Mr. Wyndham, who used to teach Auto Mechanics at the high school. His wife was the business teacher, covering accounting and typing, and she was Philip's favorite teacher.

When I asked Mrs. Wyndham about my mother, she said, "She cared about those students, and they knew it. I still remember how upset they were when they thought she'd been fired over those books."

"I wanted to ask you about that. Did you think she was wrong to bring them into the classroom?"

"It was only the last one that was an issue. The one about Malcolm X."

"Why was that?"

"Parents thought reading about him would make their children get violent, and they didn't want that. They were afraid."

"Afraid of what?"

"That they'd get in trouble, maybe even get hurt."

"Did you go to the meeting when my mom told everyone that the books had nothing to do with us leaving?"

"'Course I did. Everyone did."

"What did she say?"

"That you'd been beaten up and you had to go for the safety of the boys and the town."

"What happened then?"

"Everybody started crying. That's what happened."

"Did the students read the books after we left?"

"I suppose so. They were walking around with copies of *Soul on Ice.*"

That surprised me. Eldridge Cleaver's book was not one of the ones my mother tried to bring in. If the students were reading that, the other teachers must have not only picked up where my mother left off but also taken it even further.

After we said good-bye to the Wyndhams, Clarence drove us to his childhood home to visit with his parents. When we arrived, we found that the air-conditioning unit was broken and his wheelchair-bound, ninety-four-year-old mother had been sitting in a hot, humid room all day, not wanting to disturb him by calling for help. Despite clearly having been weakened by the experience, she perked up when she saw us and responded warmly when I walked over to hug her hello.

We first turned to talking about my parents. She stated over and over again how much good they had done for the town in general and for her family in particular. Mr. Holmes arrived a few minutes later. He stared at me from the doorway and said, "I know who you are." Then he held out his arms for a hug. As we embraced, he said into my left ear, "My bid is two spades," harking back to the time when he and his wife and my parents were bridge partners, playing sometimes at our home and sometimes at theirs.

It occurred to me that he must have thought I was my mother. Before I could explain, he stopped hugging me and pushed me back a little to look at me. Then he said, "If I'd realized you weren't your mother, I wouldn't have been so fresh." He told us later that while we were hugging, it gradually dawned on him that Aura couldn't still be fifty while he had reached ninety-four.

We also talked of their children, and I learned that my father, soon after we left Mound Bayou, had made arrangements for their oldest son to attend Tufts University, where he majored in engineering. Their next son, Cornell, who had been such a lively member of my mom's classes, had passed away from an illness several years earlier.

Then I turned to a question that had been haunting me. I was counting on Mr. and Mrs. Holmes to give me an honest answer. I wanted to know whether we had been welcome in town, or if folks had objected to our being there.

"There were some who didn't want any white folk moving in, but I helped them to understand that it was a good idea."

"How did you do that?"

"Your daddy's boss, Dr. Geiger, he flew me and a couple of others up to Boston and showed us around a clinic he'd built there."

"Columbia Point."

"That's right. We liked what we saw."

"So you came back and told everyone they should let my father come build a clinic."

"Well, we didn't know that it was your daddy back then. It was Dr. Geiger and some other man with an unusual name."

"Count Gibson?"

"Yes. They'd found some federal money to help out, and Tufts University was going to take care of everything else. We needed them here, and that's what I told people."

"And they listened to you?"

"Most did. Of course, there were some folks that didn't want anything to do with folk from the North."

"Especially white folk?"

"Yes. Some said that Tufts should just give us the money and we'd hire black doctors to come help. They said we could fix up the old Taborian Hospital instead of doing something new."

"But you didn't agree?"

"I didn't really know enough to agree or disagree. But they had accomplished something very good up there in Boston, so I thought it would be good to let them at least give it a try."

"Did you feel the same way about the books my mom tried to bring into her classroom? Did you think she was right to give them a try?"

Mrs. Holmes rejoined the conversation at that point. "I remember that lots of people were upset about that."

"Was it just the Malcolm X book, or the others too?" Elizabeth asked, remembering what Mrs. Wyndham had said about that.

"They didn't like the book by Dr. King either. People were afraid there'd be trouble."

"What kind of trouble?"

"Oh, you know—the kids acting up, making waves."

"My mom was worried when she got so much resistance; she thought maybe it wasn't right. She even went to talk with Aaron Henry about it to get his advice."

"Who's that?" asked Elizabeth.

"He was the president of the Mississippi chapter of the NAACP," I answered.

Before I could add anything more about it, Mr. Holmes jumped back in, saying, "You know, he and I used to play baseball together back in high school. We were pretty good." Another surprise. I'd known that Mr. Holmes was well respected in town, but I hadn't known that he'd gone to Boston to represent the town in evaluating the group from Tufts, nor had I known that he'd been buddies with one of the famous civil rights workers from the 1960s.

AS WE DROVE AWAY from his parents' home, Clarence said, "Joey, are you sure you still want to meet up with Pitch?" He was the ringleader of the four boys who beat me up when I was eleven.

"Absolutely."

"All right, then. He's a security guard and wants you to come see him where he works."

"Let's do this."

With that, Clarence drove to a small bank on the road between Mound Bayou and Cleveland. Pitch was waiting for us. As soon as we drove into the parking lot, he started to walk toward the van. I knew him immediately. He was still tall and lanky, but now his hair was mostly gray and his face boasted wrinkles. Yet he still managed to look handsome, his uniform creating an air of responsibility. It wasn't until I got out of the van and got close that I noticed the gun holstered on his hip and his breath smelling slightly of alcohol.

Not waiting for introductions, Pitch got right to the point. "Joey, I want to apologize for what I did."

I'm glad I'd practiced what to say next; otherwise, I might have gotten too choked up to speak. "It's been a lifetime since then, Pitch. We're different people now. I forgave you years ago."

Then I did something I hadn't planned on. I hugged him. He just stood there awkwardly, not knowing how to respond.

Clarence broke the silence, saying, "Why don't you two sit in my van to talk? It's a little more private, and you can keep the AC going."

"That's a good idea," said Pitch, reaching for the door on the driver's side. "The system in the bank is busted, and it's really hot in there."

I climbed in next to Pitch as he turned on the engine so we could have air-conditioning. Then, with his hands on the wheel and staring through the windshield as if driving down the highway, he said, "I really am sorry for what we did to you."

"I know you are," I answered, keeping my voice under control. Why was I feeling sorry for him?

We sat in uncomfortable silence for a few moments. I watched Elizabeth and Clarence standing outside the bank, laughing and talking as if this were an everyday occurrence. Finally, Pitch said, "Clarence says y'all want to know what happened that day."

"Yeah. Mostly I want to know why you did that to me."

"You want to know why?"

"I do. What made you do it?"

"We was just hanging and saw you and Thigpen in the tree house. I remember saying, 'Let's go rub us some of that.'"

"That was it? You weren't trying to make us leave town?"

"What?"

"Father Guidry thought you were trying to scare us into leaving town. He even said you might have been paid to attack me."

"It wasn't nothin' like that. We was just messin' around."

I didn't answer.

"But you didn't want us to. You kept trying to push our hands away, like this." At that point, he started flailing his hands all over the place, mimicking how I must have acted that day. "We never tried to hurt you. You was just pushing me away so hard that you fell out of the tree."

I may have had a concussion and may not remember everything, but I know that's not what happened. He hit me repeatedly to get me to stop resisting him, pulverizing my thigh and leaving it one purple mass from the knee to the hip. Although I remembered the incident differently than Pitch did, I decided not to challenge his recollection, figuring he avoided feeling guilty by believing that it had all been some misunderstanding. Instead, I said, "Do you know why we left town?"

When he didn't answer, I said, "Father Guidry told my parents we had to leave because if word got out to the Ku Klux Klan and the White Citizens' Council that four black boys had molested a white girl, they'd kill the four of you and burn down the town. He figured if we left as quickly as we could, that was less likely to happen."

"I never knew that."

"Didn't you wonder why we left so suddenly?"

"'Cause people said we raped you."

"That made me not want to go to school. But I don't think my folks would have left if that's all it was."

"We didn't rape you," Pitch said, not really hearing my comment. "We didn't do anything that bad," he added, shaking his head.

"You don't get it, do you? Do you have any daughters?"

"Yes," he said. "And I see where you're going with that. If anybody did to my daughters like I did you, I'd kill 'em."

"That's how my dad felt about you."

"But why was everyone saying that we raped you?"

"I don't know. I guess people want to believe the worst. My mother tried to tell everyone at school what had happened. She said flat out that I hadn't been raped."

"Yeah, I remember that."

"You were at the high school when she spoke?"

"Yeah. I was there."

"You went to school that day, after everything that happened?"

"Yeah. Didn't see no reason not to go. When your momma talked, half the students were crying and the other half were staring at me, really mad."

"Then what happened?"

"They blamed me for making your mom leave."

"We were going to leave at the end of the year in any case. That's why my dad was out of town. He was interviewing for a new job."

"All the same, your mom must really hate me."

"Not anymore. Even at the time, she said that she didn't want you punished. She wanted you taught."

"Well, Father Guidry didn't believe that. He threw George out of St. Gabriel's. Wouldn't let him go back."

"We didn't know that. I'm sorry."

"You're saying 'I'm sorry' to me?"

"I am. You were kids. I never wanted anything bad to happen to you."

"Well, I'm sorry too. We never meant to hurt you. I didn't even know we did until we heard you'd been taken to the clinic."

"It's over, Pitch. It's been over for a long time."

Then, miraculously, we chatted like old friends. He told me about his work as a security guard, how he'd been shot three times. He said that one of his brothers had become a math teacher. He spoke about his children. I told him about mine. And then it was time to go. My journey back in time was over.

EPILOGUE

Jo (56 years old)

My mother died shortly after her ninety-first birthday, vital to the end. She had slowed down a bit—her short-term memory wasn't what it used to be, and she had more and more senior moments—but she remained a role model for all of us. Mound Bayou was the beginning of a long and successful teaching career that eventually took her to the inner cities of Miami and Los Angeles. She was passionate about politics, frequently participated in marches for civil and gay rights, and was a member of Parents, Families and Friends of Lesbians and Gays (PFLAG), the National Organization for Women (NOW), and the Democratic Party.

While working full-time, she earned a master's degree in education at the University of Miami. By the time she retired, twenty years later, she had developed an international reputation for teaching Shakespeare at some of the most underprivileged schools in the country. This work was dramatized in the made-for-TV movie *Hard Lessons*.

My oldest sister, Connie, is a retired town planner and lives in Amherst, Massachusetts. Philip attended law school and works for Los Alamos National Laboratory. Charles, after dropping out of school at fourteen, earned a graduate degree in theater arts and is a well-respected art and theater critic, known in San Francisco as The Storming Bohemian. My father remarried a year after my parents' divorce. His wife, Audrey Reid, was a fellow pediatrician. She and their two daughters, my sisters Ruth-Anne Thornton and Leondra Hauck, brought him great happiness until his death eight years ago. And I became a writer. Not at first. I held a wide range of roles in the transportation and high-tech industries before deciding to stay at home and focus on family. I married my college sweetheart, Jon Ivester, and we have four children. When my youngest started school, I became a substitute math teacher and eventually a college professor. My mother, after retiring from teaching at age sixty-five, moved in with us and helped raise our children, enriching their lives, as she did mine.

ACKNOWLEDGMENTS

The first person I want to thank is my mother, Aura Kruger. Without her courage, this book would never have been written. She followed my father, Leon Kruger, on his idealistic quest and made his dream her own. Devoted to teaching for over twenty years, she labored ceaselessly to help her students achieve their potential. In so doing, she achieved her own, in the process gaining independence and self-confidence.

I am grateful to several individuals who reviewed my many drafts with an editorial eye, patiently teaching me the craft, transforming me from a proficient business writer to a real author. Alexandra Shelley is the editor who took me on as a client only after I recognized that I was at the beginning of the project, not the end. Michael Mitchell is the dramaturgist who stepped outside his usual field of dramatic works to advise me regarding when the pace slackened and when I needed to dig deeper. Greg Durham is the fellow author who built my confidence when I worried that my writing wasn't worthy of publication. Bob Williamson is the mystery writer who suggested I emulate his genre by tightening up the beginning and end of each chapter. Evan Karp, the executive director of Quiet Lightning, encouraged me to move beyond my mother's story and tell more of my own.

Before completing my own acknowledgments, I'd like to present those that my mother penned when she first finished her journal. She wrote:

I want to thank my former husband, Leon Kruger, who helped me develop my self-confidence and overcome my shyness, who shared with me four children, and who led me to the cotton fields of Mississippi where I began my teaching career in earnest. If his efforts to be Don Quixote hadn't inspired me, many of the events described in this book could not have happened.

My four children helped, each in their own way. My oldest, Connie, asked that I write about her adoption, thus launching me down the path to becoming an author. Philip, my older son, has encouraged me even though he finds it unnerving to have anecdotes about him recorded for others to read. Charles, my younger son, gave me the book *The Artist's Way*, confident it would motivate me to begin writing when I was having difficulty getting started. As usual, I've mentioned my children in order of their births, and thus Jo, the youngest, comes last. Without her help, there would have been no book, only notes for my extended family. It was she who took my early scribbles and patiently worked with me to turn them into a cohesive story, rapidly evolving from helpful assistant to co-author.

My children-in-law, Jon Ivester and Susan Tracy, and my nephews, Stephen Kramer and Bennett Lerner, each commented on the growing manuscript. My granddaughter, Elizabeth Norman, helped edit some of my work, and all of my nieces and nephews and grandchildren and great-grandchildren have been wonderfully supportive.

I thank Karen Hughes, one of my first friends in Texas. She encouraged me to write when she heard my stories, and later introduced me to her editor.

Barbara Malley, who knew me when I was eleven, has reviewed every sentence for grammatical mistakes, overused words, and trite phrases. Her occasional "Wow!" or "Good for you, Aura!" did much to boost my confidence.

There are the friends I found through book clubs who have offered inestimable help, Joy, Peggy, Justin, Brook, Jo, Landon, Sandy, Claire, and Dave. There are my bridge partners, teaching colleagues, and fellow Bums Table members, especially Ann, Joyce W., Mary, Eleanor, Frances, David, Joyce B., Gary, George, Nancy, Jeannie, Buck, BB, Sue, Myrtle, and Tony; and my friend Deborah Brouse, the woman who helped me develop my independence when I found myself alone at fifty-one. And to all the others who influenced my life along the way, who helped mold me to become the person I am today, my humble thanks.

I share my mother's gratitude to all of these people. In addition, I must mention the very special person who made it possible for me to return to Mound Bayou with my daughter, Elizabeth. Clarence Holmes spent weeks setting up interviews, guided my decisions regarding how to spend my time, hosted us in his home, and shared with me the remarkable experience of revisiting my childhood.

In closing, there are too many wonderful friends for me to list here, but I want to thank Gail, Barbara, and Beth, the first of my friends to suggest that I use my mother's journals as a platform from which to write my own book focusing on our two years in Mississippi; Forrest, who graciously spent many hours helping to publicize my work; my two younger sisters, Ruth and Leondra; and their mother, Audrey.

Finally, I have to thank my immediate family—my husband, Jon, and my four children, Elizabeth, Ben, Jeremy, and Sammy —who have listened to my endless chatter about the book and encouraged me every step of the way.

About the Author

photo credit: KerryLDphotography

JO IVESTER spent two years of her childhood living in a trailer in Mound Bayou, where she was the only white student at her junior high. She finished high school in Florida before attending Reed, MIT, and Stanford in preparation for a career in transportation and manufacturing. Following the birth of her fourth child, she became a teacher. She and her husband teach each January at MIT and travel extensively, splitting their time between Texas, Colorado, and Singapore.

SELECTED TITLES FROM SHE WRITES PRESS

She Writes Press is an independent publishing company
founded to serve women writers everywhere.
Visit us at www.shewritespress.com.

Times They Were A-Changing: Women Remember the '60s & '70s
edited by Kate Farrell, Amber Lea Starfire, and Linda Joy Myers.
$16.95, 978-1-938314-04-9. Forty-eight powerful stories and
poems detailing the breakthrough moments experienced by
women during the '60s and '70s.

Tasting Home: Coming of Age in the Kitchen by Judith Newton.
$16.95, 978-1-938314-03-2. An extraordinary journey through
the cuisines, cultures, and politics of the 1940s through 2011,
complete with recipes.

Dearest Ones at Home: Clara Taylor's Letters from Russia, 1917-1919
edited by Katrina Maloney and Patricia Maloney. Clara Taylor's
detailed, delightful letters documenting her two years in Russia
teaching factory girls self-sufficiency skills—right in the middle
of World War I.

The Coconut Latitudes: Secrets, Storms, and Survival in the Caribbean
by Rita Gardner. $16.95, 978-1-63152-901-6. A haunting, lyrical
memoir about a dysfunctional family's experiences in a reality far
from the envisioned Eden—and the terrible cost of keeping
secrets.

Renewable: One Woman's Search for Simplicity, Faithfulness, and Hope
by Eileen Flanagan. $16.95, 978-1-63152-968-9. At age forty-
nine, Eileen Flanagan had an aching feeling that she wasn't living
up to her youthful ideals or potential, so she started trying to
change the world—and in doing so, she found the courage to
change her life.

100 Under $100: One Hundred Tools for Empowering Global Women
by Betsy Teutsch. $29.95, 978-1-63152-934-4. An inspiring,
comprehensive look at the many tools being employed today to
empower women in the developing world and help them raise
themselves out of poverty.